JESUS IN THE 9 TO 5

FACING THE CHALLENGES OF TODAY'S BUSINESS WORLD

DENNIS E. HENSLEY, PHD

AMG Publishers

**Jesus in the 9 to 5:
Facing the Challenges of Today's Business World**

Copyright © 2013 by Dennis E. Hensley, PhD

Published by AMG Publishers, Inc. 6815 Shallowford Rd. Chattanooga, Tennessee 37421

Published in association with MacGregor Literary Agency, PO Box 1316, Manzanita, OR 97130

All rights reserved. Except for brief quotations in printed reviews, no part of this publication may be reproduced, stored in a retrieval system, or transmitted in any form or by any means (printed, written, photocopied, visual electronic, audio, or otherwise) without the prior permission of the publisher.

This work contains elements of fiction. Names, characters, places, and incidents either are the product of the author's imagination or are used fictitiously. Any resemblance to actual persons, either living or dead, events, or locales is entirely coincidental.

First Printing—September 2013

Print edition	ISBN 13: 978-0-89957-179-9
EPUB edition	ISBN 13: 978-1-61715-409-6
Mobi edition	ISBN 13: 978-1-61715-410-2
ePDF edition	ISBN 13: 978-1-61715-411-9

Cover layout and design by Kent Jensen at Knail, LLC, Salem, OR

Editing by Rich Cairnes and Rick Steele

Interior design and typesetting by Kristin Goble, PerfecType, Nashville, TN

Printed in the United States of America
18 17 16 15 14 13 –QG– 6 5 4 3 2 1

Contents

Section 1: How Jesus Handled Personnel Problems 1
Section 2: How Jesus Recruited and Trained Personnel 13
Section 3: How Jesus Revealed His Success Principles 25
Section 4: Jesus on Closing a Sale 35
Section 5: Jesus on Quality Control 47
Section 6: Jesus on Setting and Reaching Goals 63
Section 7: What Jesus Taught about Diversified Portfolios 83
Section 8: Jesus on Accepting a Personal Calling 91
Section 9: Time Management Concepts Shared by Jesus 107
Section 10: Jesus on Humility, Accumulation, and Independence 121
Section 11: What Jesus Taught about Stress Management 143
Section 12: Jesus on Discipline, Appearance, and Prayer 169

Section 1

HOW JESUS HANDLED PERSONNEL PROBLEMS

Jesus Christ walked into Decker's Bar and Grill and waited for his eyes to adjust to the darkness. Mickey the bartender turned to offer a greeting, but Jesus held up one hand for silence. He scanned the bar, spotted his target, and moved forward.

Pete Fishers slowly lifted his head when Jesus slid into the booth, across the table from him. Pete's bloodshot eyes squinted.

"Do I know you?" Pete half slurred. A bottle of wine, two-thirds empty, rested near his elbow.

"You're about to," said Jesus. He picked up the wine bottle, looked at it, grimaced, squeezed it for a moment, then set it back on the table. "I understand you need a job."

Pete rubbed one hand over his unshaven face. Cautiously, he asked, "Wha' you want? You with the IRS or something?" He groped for the wine and took a big swig straight from the bottle. He swallowed, then blanched, as though poisoned.

"Ugh! You call that wine?" he yelled at the bartender. "It's like water."

Instinctively, Mickey reached for a new bottle, but Jesus turned and shook his head. Mickey halted in mid-reach, returned the gaze, then retracted his hand. He grabbed a rag and busied himself wiping the bar.

Jesus turned back to Pete. "I have a job I need you to do."

Pete took a moment to size up the man across from him. "Who sent you?"

Jesus smiled slowly. "We'll talk about that sometime. For now, however, we need to get you out of here. Follow me." Jesus rose from the booth.

Pete sat another moment, then hunched his shoulders. He made a clumsy, noisy effort to get to his feet. "Sure . . . sure, just like that," he mumbled under his breath. He tried to snap his fingers but couldn't coordinate the effort. "Follow the stranger. Why not? Prob'ly 'bout to be tossed out of here anyway." He fumbled in his pants pocket, withdrew his wallet, opened it, and found it empty.

"Slight problem," he said, holding out the empty wallet. "Broke."

Jesus nodded toward a stuffed trout mounted on a nearby wall. "Go over there and reach into that fish's mouth."

Pete smiled sardonically. "You're kidding, right? You're drunker than I am."

"Trust me," said Jesus. "Do it."

Reluctantly, haltingly, Pete swayed across the room toward the trophy fish. He pointed at it, and Jesus nodded. Shaking his head, Pete pushed his thumb and forefinger into the fish's open mouth. He felt an obstruction. It was a wadded piece of paper. He removed it and began to unfold it as he retraced his steps to Jesus.

"It's a fifty dollar bill," he said with genuine amazement. "How'd you do that?"

"Give it to the bartender, and let's leave," said Jesus.

HOW JESUS HANDLED PERSONNEL PROBLEMS

Pete frowned. "Fifty bucks? No way. I'm due some serious change."

Jesus turned him toward the bar and pushed him. "You're about to experience serious change."

Three minutes later, out on the sidewalk, Pete raised a hand to shield his blinded eyes. He put his other hand out to steady himself against a building.

"Whoa, partner," he said. "I appreciate you covering my tab in there, but I need to get my bearings. Who exactly are you, and what were you saying about a job?"

"I'm starting a furniture business," said Jesus. "Handmade desks, chairs, tables. I need a general foreman. You're good with your hands, and you're a natural leader . . . when you're sober. You've been fired three times for drinking. That's now at an end. From now on you're working for me. You're my company's new honcho."

Pete stood transfixed for a moment. "How do you know so much about me? Why're you willing to give me another chance?"

"Everyone has fallen short at one time or another," said Jesus. "I see your potential."

"I do need a job . . ."

"You need a whole new life," corrected Jesus. "I've come to give you that."

"Furniture, eh?"

"I grew up with a saw in my hands. We're going to take that to new levels."

Pete shrugged, then drew in a deep breath, trying to stay focused. "I'm grateful. Really. I am. I promise you, I'll never let you down."

Jesus shook his head slightly. "We'll face that issue another time." He took a moment to look around. "Right now, we need to get some other men. How about your brother?"

"Andy? Hmmm . . . sure. He's been looking for work. I can call him."

"Do that," said Jesus, "tonight. For now, come with me. We need an accountant and finance director. I know just the guy. He works for the IRS, but I think we can convince him to join us."

"The IRS?" said Pete, pulling up short. "I hate those guys. I had my own general contracting company once. Those guys came in and padlocked my doors and put me out of business."

"It was your own fault," said Jesus flatly. "You didn't pay your quarterly estimated taxes, you hired people off the books, and you tried to deduct personal expenses as business purchases. You have to render to the government what is owed to the government."

"How do you know . . . ?"

"Look at me," Jesus interrupted, suddenly moving in until they were face-to-face. "Look at me!"

Pete stood absolutely still.

"Do I look like someone who has no understanding of people?"

"No . . . no, sir," said Pete, dry-mouthed. He studied the face of Jesus.

"Trust your judgment, Pete. Look at me. Who do you think I am?"

Pete paused, then said solemnly, "You're the boss. You're the guy in charge." He nodded slowly. "And I'm okay with that. Sure enough, yeah, you're the boss."

Jesus smiled. "I knew I made a good choice with you. I can build the whole company on you. Let's go."

HOW JESUS HANDLED PERSONNEL PROBLEMS

Please read the following question twice, then sit for a few minutes thinking carefully about an answer: Would Jesus be a hard person to work for?

I was asked this question by a friend while we were eating lunch together. He was having problems with two of his employees. One new secretary couldn't type a memo or letter without making at least two spelling errors on each page. And one of the sales reps was not following up on some of the client leads assigned to him by my friend.

My friend had counseled these two people, had taught them how to do better work, and had explained the benefits for the company and for the employees of "a job well done." Nevertheless, the employees continued to do substandard work.

"I want my office to do excellent work for our parent company," my friend told me, "yet, in order to get things done the right way, I wind up acting like a tyrant. Sometimes I get so frustrated about their slipshod work, I yell at them.

"That's no way for a Christian to behave. I just keep wondering how Jesus would have handled a situation like this. Do you think he would be a hard person to work for?"

Christ's Problems

"The situation at your office is mild compared to the management problems Jesus faced," I assured him. "Your secretary, Cindy, can't spell. What's that compared with working with a guy like Judas plotting behind your back to have you killed?

"And your salesman, Ted, won't expand his customer base. What's that compared with having a guy like Peter traveling with you, knowing he may pull out a sword and try to kill anyone who disagrees with you?"

My friend smiled. "Okay, so maybe my problems aren't that extreme—but they're still frustrating. How can I be a patient and gracious Christian, yet still produce good work for my company? It's tough being a manager when people don't live up to your expectations."

"I'm sure Jesus would agree with you," I said. "Christ spent more than three years teaching his disciples, advising them, counseling them, empowering them, yet they still let him down in the end. Jesus revived Peter's mother-in-law, yet Peter later denied three times that he even knew Jesus. Jesus had the disciples distribute the food when his miracle enabled five thousand people to be fed, yet these same disciples couldn't even stay awake long enough to pray with Jesus in the garden of Gethsemane. Jesus predicted he would rise from the dead—and he did!—but Thomas wouldn't believe it until he touched Christ's wounds."

Positive Results

"You're only underscoring what I said before," my friend replied. "It's hard to be a boss when people you work with let you down. And I'll agree that my management problems seem petty when compared with Christ's. Still . . . there's one big difference."

"What's that?"

"The results," said my friend. "Despite the failures of the people who worked with him, Jesus still managed to build a team of workers who reached the goals he had set. They established churches. They preached the gospel all over the world. They mentored younger men and women to carry on after them. They wrote books of the New Testament—they achieved great things in spite of their failures.

"And that's the big difference. My workers aren't achieving anything. I could be more tolerant of their shortcomings if I could just see some overall progress. But I *don't* see it, and that makes me discouraged and angry."

"You can't give up," I said. "Training and encouraging people are never-ending processes. But I think Jesus used two approaches you haven't picked up on yet. That's probably why his people succeeded, whereas yours haven't."

"Two approaches? What two approaches? I'm willing to try anything at this point."

Praise Effort

"If you look closely at the way Jesus worked with his disciples," I said, "you'll see two things. First, rather than always point out the mistakes of his disciples, he chose instead to catch them doing things right and praise their efforts.

"For example, when Peter became the first disciple to recognize Jesus as the long-awaited Messiah, Jesus honored Peter's faith by saying that Peter's confession would be the foundation upon which the church would be established. This was positive reinforcement and positive motivation."

"But I do that with my employees," my friend insisted.

"No," I countered. "You may think you do, but you really don't. Every time you call Cindy into your office and say, 'You've done it again, Cindy. You've made more spelling errors in this letter,' that sends a message to her you're expecting her to fail. So, she does. You haven't motivated her to do otherwise."

"Well, how do you think Jesus would do it?" my friend challenged me.

"I think that each time Cindy typed something that was flawless," I shared, "he would call her in and say that such excellent work reflected well on the whole image of the company, and that Cindy seemed to be getting better each day at her work. This would make Cindy feel like a real part of the team, a valued colleague. It would inspire her to try to produce another flawless letter so she could feel good again about herself and her work."

Restate Goals

"All right, I can buy that—in theory," said my friend. But what happens when she starts to slip again? Workers are never continually excellent in what they do. Sooner or later they start to get lax again."

"Unfortunately, that's true," I had to agree, "but that's where Christ's second approach comes in. Whenever his disciples would seem to grow weary or lose their momentum or have doubts about their work, Jesus would restate his goals and objectives for them and remind them of the worthiness of their mission.

"I want to read a passage to you that may amaze you," I said. I pulled a New Testament from my pocket. "After working three years with his disciples and then rising from the dead, Jesus still had to contend with people who were dubious about his power and identity. He dealt with this by ignoring their doubts, focusing instead on the restatement of the overall mission." I read Matthew 28:16-20 to him:

> Then the eleven disciples went to Galilee, to the mountain where Jesus had told them to go. When they saw him, they worshiped him; but some doubted. Then Jesus came

become part of the foundation upon which the Lord would build his church?"

"Right. Like we said before, Peter was the first disciple to proclaim Jesus to be the Son of God."

"True. Yet, despite this great faith, it was Peter who later denied three times he even *knew* Jesus. For all intents and purposes, Peter's ministry should have been finished right then. But Jesus did something to show Peter he had forgiven him and that he still had confidence in him."

My friend leaned forward and watched closely as I located two verses in my Bible.

"Here in Luke 24:34 and again over here in 1 Corinthians 15:5, it says that after Jesus rose from the dead he appeared to Simon Peter even before he met with the Emmaus disciples or the other ten apostles or any of the multitudes. He made meeting with Peter one of his top priorities. He reestablished their original bonds. He put Peter's disappointing failure behind them. In a very real sense, he recommissioned Peter to the work of the ministry."

My friend nodded. "And Peter preached a sermon at Pentecost that was dynamic enough to lead three thousand people to salvation. What a turnaround. Amazing!"

"Yes, but not unbelievable," I said. "The power was there in Peter all along. It just took the forgiveness of Christ and the reaffirmation of his confidence and trust to bring it out."

"And you think if Ted could forgive me for my unreasonable expectations, we *both* could get back on the right track and focus on some *challenging but realistic* goals?"

"Ted needs to know you still believe in him and his abilities," I said. "You, however, also need to know that Ted still believes in your abilities and your strategy for crossing the finish line. You two can accomplish your mutual goals *if* you follow Jesus' example with Peter—forgive, then reaffirm."

My friend grabbed the bill. "My treat," he said. "You've given me a lot to think about. Let's get together again tomorrow."

"Tomorrow?"

"Uh-huh. We'll meet here again, okay? And I'll bring Ted along. I want you to meet him. I'll let you be a witness to the way I'll be bragging about his good work. You know . . . reaffirming him."

"Good," I said. "And while you *reaffirm*, let's hope Ted can *forgive*."

"Forgive?" asked my friend.

"Forgive us both," I said, "for sticking him with the check."

Section 2

How Jesus Recruited and Trained Personnel

It is said the fastest way to determine whether a person is an optimist or a pessimist is to hand him an eight-ounce glass containing four ounces of water. If he says it's half full, he's an optimist. If he says it's half empty, he's a pessimist.

One of my college professors conducted this experiment on me one day in class. After handing me the glass, he asked, "Are you an optimist or a pessimist?"

"Neither," I replied. "I'm an opportunist."

I then drank the water.

Multiplication Tables

I'm convinced that Jesus was an opportunist. He always seemed to focus on what people *had* rather than what they *lacked*. He also tried to teach this lesson to his disciples.

After preaching all day on a mountainside, Jesus paused to rest. His disciples came to him and said the large crowd of listeners was hungry. The disciples didn't know what to do about this because there were five thousand men, plus women and children, in need of bread, but the disciples didn't have five thousand loaves to give them.

Jesus' response was that of a true opportunist. He asked, "How many loaves do you have?" (Mark 6:38).

Now, I really like that. I like it because I think it's the same question Jesus is asking all believers yet today. He isn't interested in our excuses or our whining or our blame-shifting or our false humility or our inadequacies. Instead, he's interested in our efforts to serve him with whatever capabilities we have and in whatever circumstances we find ourselves.

With Jesus, there are no A and B teams. He doesn't have first- and second-string people. To Jesus, the servant who doubles the two talents is no less praiseworthy than the servant who doubles the five talents. To Jesus, that's equal effort. It's the person who complains about having only one talent, and therefore does nothing, whom Jesus calls the "wicked, lazy servant" (Matthew 25:26).

Little Big Man

The point we miss is that God often purposely seeks the least gifted people to do his bidding. He does this as a way of emphasizing that it is God at work, not man.

Could little David have slain giant Goliath without God's help? Of course not. Could Joshua have crumbled the massive walls of Jericho without God's help? Don't be ridiculous. Could Moses have separated the Red Sea, could Elijah have called down fire from heaven, could Peter have raised the dead, without God's help? No, no, most emphatically no!

HOW JESUS RECRUITED AND TRAINED PERSONNEL

Who were these people? They were nobodies: a shepherd boy, a desert wayfarer, a fallen prince, a penniless prophet, an uneducated fisherman. These people had no prestige, no money, no political influence. And that was one of the chief reasons God chose them as his spokesmen and ministers. Anyone observing the miracles wrought by these common men would have had to say, "Surely, this is the *hand of God* at work."

Nowhere is this more evident than in the calling of Gideon, whom God selected to strike down the Midianites. Even Gideon couldn't believe it. "Pardon me, my lord," Gideon replied, "but how can I save Israel? My clan is the weakest in Manasseh, and I am the least in my family" (Judges 6:15). In God's eyes, these were perfect credentials, for nothing about Gideon smacked of a general's bearing or countenance. God was the real commander.

Poor Gideon. So skeptical of his calling was he, he had to double check *twice* with God about it through the spreading of the wool fleece. However, once he was convinced, he raised an army of thirty-two thousand combat soldiers. Ironically, once Gideon was finally ready to go into battle, God wasn't.

Gideon had missed the point. If thirty-two thousand Jewish warriors attacked the Midianites and won, they would think they had gained the victory by their own power. So, God reduced the force to a mere three hundred handpicked soldiers and inspired Gideon to use a psychological ploy that so terrified the Midianites, they began to kill each other. Gideon and his small band of warriors were able to defeat the one hundred thirty-five thousand men of the Midianites (Judges 8:10). Some one hundred twenty thousand Midianites died and the other fifteen thousand fled.

After this great victory, the people tried to make Gideon their ruler. Gideon, however, responded, "I will not rule over you, nor will my son rule over you. The LORD will rule over you" (Judges 8:23). Gideon knew he was still the young, poor, inexperienced fellow he had been before the battle. Only God had made the difference. As such, God deserved the credit and homage, not Gideon.

What Do *You* Have?

The Bible is filled with stories of people who used whatever they had at hand to serve God. One widow gave her last bit of meal and oil to God's prophet Elijah. In return, she was given a never-ending supply of meal and oil (1 Kings 17:13-16). Another widow gave two mites, a financial pittance, yet all she had. Christ praised her gift as being more worthy than even the most valuable of the other gifts donated (Luke 21:2-3).

In these and other situations, the Lord was more concerned about the attitude of the individual than with his or her ability. God's people succeeded because they were willing to make the most of whatever they had. They were opportunists.

How about you? Are you an opportunist? Have you paused lately to count how many loaves *you* have on hand? Perhaps you've forgotten you have spiritual gifts capable of accomplishing significant things for Christ. If you have, I have a suggestion: Fill an eight-ounce glass with four ounces of water. Look at it a moment. Then throw the water in your face. Wake yourself up to the opportunities around you.

How Jesus Trains

Years ago when my daughter Jeanette was just learning her numbers, I found I could keep her occupied and quiet for hours by giving her coloring books with dot-to-dot pages in them.

HOW JESUS RECRUITED AND TRAINED PERSONNEL

"What is *this* picture?" she'd ask, holding up a page of random dots.

"I don't know," I'd admit. "You'll have to connect all the dots in the right order before we'll be able to see the finished picture. Can you do it?"

She would smile, nod, then grab a crayon and begin slowly, painstakingly drawing lines from one dot to the next. At first, she had some problems: sometimes the numbers would run higher than she could count; other times, she'd confuse twelve with twenty-one and would connect the dots out of order.

I recall seeing some very bizarre dot connections in those first couple of books she worked on—buildings that resembled snowmen, cars that looked like caterpillars, and one particular airplane that came out like a hot dog in a lopsided bun.

To help Jeanette see where she had gone wrong (yet not discourage her), I would pull her onto my lap, put my big hand around her little hand, and then, moving together, we would retrace the dots in the right sequence. When the building or car or airplane then came out looking the way it should, Jeanette felt she'd had "a hand" in doing it right.

As my daughter grew older, we continued to work together on dot-to-dot puzzles; these puzzles, however, were from the book of life rather than a coloring book. For example, sometimes Jeanette would make poor decisions about television shows she would watch or she'd disappoint friends in some way or she'd forget to do her homework.

Each of these "misconnections" would distort the picture of what Jeanette was supposed to be like. We would have to backtrack to where the wrong connection had been made and decide what the connection should have been. (Today, she is a wife, mother, and elementary music teacher, and I'm very pleased with how her picture has turned out.)

If I have been wise in helping my daughter learn how to "connect" her life properly, it is only because Jesus set the example for me. I, too, have made many poor connections in my life that have altered and distorted the perfect picture that Christ would have me be. In many instances, he has put his big hand around my little hand and helped me to retrace the connections the correct way.

Sometimes the Lord helps me retrace my life by sending another Christian to counsel or admonish me. For instance, many years ago, I was attending graduate school and working two jobs. Sunday morning was the only time I could sleep late, so I missed Sunday school for about a month. Then one day my wife gently said, "You're my husband, Dennis. You're supposed to set an example for me." She was right. I've never missed a Sunday school class since then except for extreme illness.

Other times the Lord helps me correct misconnections by exposing me to specific passages of Scripture. One time a Christian business associate of mine and I were trying to land a contract to provide some specialized training for a large company. The man we met with was an abrasive, foul-mouthed individual.

After enduring this man's off-color remarks for half an hour, my friend told him that we found his language offensive. He asked if the man could please refrain from swearing while we talked. The man promptly showed us the door, and we lost the account.

Although I said nothing to my friend about his decision to speak up, I secretly wished he would have waited until *after* we had signed the contracts. That night, however, I was preparing a devotion and, inadvertently, I came across these verses: "Do not envy the wicked, do not desire their company; for their hearts plot violence, and their lips talk about making trouble" (Proverbs 24:1-2). I realized instantly that my friend had done the wise thing in separating us from that man and his company. A week later we were hired by a much more prestigious firm offering an even better contract.

The Lord uses many other ways to help me connect the dots of my life in proper sequence. Sometimes it's through a sermon or a hymn or a Bible commentary or an article in a Christian periodical. Other times it's through a Christian book, a film, someone's testimony, or just a quiet time of prayer and meditation. Whatever the way, he lets me know when I've used the wrong crayon or transposed the dot numbers.

And he lets me have "a hand" in making better connections.

Pete Fishers and Jesus were seated in a conference room at the regional offices of the Internal Revenue Service. It resembled an interrogation room, which, for all intents and purposes, it often actually was. There were metal folding chairs, a pressed-wood table with metal folding legs, and in one corner a computer and screen, both turned off. The room had no windows.

"I like what they haven't done to the place," said Pete, under his breath. "It has that quaint dungeon element to it. But I guess, when in Rome . . ." Pete was a tradesman with a very limited vocabulary. He would have had no idea what the word ambiance *meant.*

". . . or Rome's dungeons," echoed Jesus.

The door opened, and a man in a three-piece brown-striped suit entered. He wore gold rimmed glasses and wing-tip shoes and sported a tightly trimmed mustache. In his arms he held several manila folders and two large white envelopes filled with papers.

"Ah, Mr. Fishers," said the man briskly. He pulled out a chair, sat, and then spread his paperwork on the table before him. "We meet again. I'm Matthew Feingold. I worked your case a year ago, you may recall."

Pete smirked. "Of all the gin joints in the world . . ."

Ignoring him, the IRS agent continued, "Our office received your call an hour ago. I've taken time to review your case, and I must tell you right up front, I see no instances in which I overlooked any details or treated you unfairly. But, obviously, you must feel differently. I see you've brought an associate this time. Your attorney? Personal accountant?"

"Neither," said Jesus, leaning slightly forward. "In fact, I, personally, don't get along all that well with lawyers and money handlers. But that's neither here nor there. Actually, this visit is about you."

The man turned slowly in his chair so as to get a better view of the stranger. "About me?"

"He's starting a furniture company," interjected Pete. "I'm the new foreman, head of production and distribution."

The agent shifted his gaze slightly. "You?" He paused, then added, "No offense, but your track record doesn't exactly portray you as management material."

"Oh, it gets crazier," said Pete. "He wants you to join us as head of finance. That's why we're here. You can put aside all those papers. This ain't about when you shut down my business. It's about putting you on a new career path."

Feingold sat back in his chair. He took a moment to look first at one man and then the other. He could see this wasn't a joke or some kind of weird prank. They were serious.

HOW JESUS RECRUITED AND TRAINED PERSONNEL

"Well, thank you," he said, briskly, "but as you can see, I already have a job."

"Why be stuck in a job when you can have a career?" asked Jesus.

The man shrugged his shoulders. "Career? Job? Aren't you splitting hairs?"

"I don't need to split them," responded Jesus. "I already know exactly how many you have."

The agent turned slowly to Pete, then asked, "Is he . . .?"

"There are 107,822," concluded Jesus.

The agent stared hard at Jesus, expecting some sort of chuckle or smile. None came. This guy wasn't kidding.

"But how could you possibly . . . ?"

"Get used to it," said Pete. "He just knows stuff. Kind of creepy, ain't it? But he's a really nice guy once you spend some time with him. So, how about it? Want to hear our offer?"

"You're really serious? You called for this appointment, and all you wanted to do was to offer me a job? You just show up like this? Most people would have asked for a résumé in advance."

Pete pointed a thumb toward Jesus. "Trust me. He ain't 'most people.'"

"I know all I need to know about you," said Jesus, drawing the agent's attention back toward himself. "You've been shy, reserved, quiet most of your life. Your two older brothers were big into sports, but you never had the build for it, nor the interest. You studied accounting in college because it was a field that would enable you to spend a lot of time alone, doing calculations and bookkeeping."

"Who told you this?" the man demanded.

Pete lifted a hand. "Save us all a lot of time, pal. Just listen to him. He's got sources like you can't believe." He nodded to Jesus and said, "Go ahead, Boss."

"Lately, however, you've begun to wonder what the point of your life is," continued Jesus, still looking the agent directly in the eyes. "You audit people, take away their homes, close their businesses, drain their savings accounts, and you feel lousy about it. Sure, it's the law, and you're good at following the letter of the law, but at the end of the day, it leaves you feeling hollow, empty, even guilty. Three weeks ago you had more than 109,000 hairs, but you've been losing them fast lately. Worry, dread, anger . . . they all take a toll."

Feingold looked back at Jesus. His forehead wrinkled, his eyes narrowed. He raised his right hand slowly to his lips. "I haven't even talked to my wife about these things."

"He cuts to the chase, don't he?" said Pete. "No use denying anything. Don't ask me how, but, like I said, he knows stuff."

"You don't have to continue hating your work," said Jesus. "You can follow me. You can help us build things—good things of high quality that will help people. You can be in on the ground floor of something new and vibrant. You'll set up our entire payroll plan. You'll manage cash flow and billings. You'll help us set prices, and you'll monitor cost of goods and services."

"This is a genuine offer?" the agent asked incredulously. "I mean, this isn't some kind of retaliation for what I did to Mr. Fishers and his business?"

"Enough of that," said Pete from the side. "My dad was Mister Fishers."

"Look carefully at me," said Jesus. He extended his hand. "I know what you need to do, the way you should go. I'll always speak truth to you. I can provide you the light you've been looking for in your dark existence. You need to walk out of here today and come with me. If you stay here, you'll die a slow death."

"And go bald in the process, so it seems," added Pete.

HOW JESUS RECRUITED AND TRAINED PERSONNEL

The agent took the hand of Jesus and squeezed. "Okay, yes, I'll join you. I can't believe I'm saying this, but, yes, I'll come and work for you." He released his handshake and turned to the door. But then, suddenly he paused, slowly turned back, needing to say something, but not knowing how to express it.

"It's hard, isn't it?" said Jesus. "I know that. You have pending cases. You're wondering what to say to your wife. And working for the government is all you've ever known. What I'm offering you is an absolute miracle, a dream come true. But you're a man of facts and figures. You're wondering if you can trust a dream. This seems too good to be true, and that makes you nervous."

Feingold lowered his gaze. "Thank you for understanding. I mean no disrespect. It's just that . . . just that . . ."

"That it requires a leap of faith," said Pete, rising from his chair. "I hear you, bro'. Two hours ago I was feeling just what you're feeling now. Don't be ashamed. Been there, felt that, amigo. But let me share something with you. You and me . . . we need this guy. I'm on the downside of everything right now. And you don't seem much better. I know we ain't cut from the same cloth, but we've got the same hang-ups. What we've been doing for the past few years ain't been gettin' us anywhere." He put a hand on Feingold's shoulder. "Come on. Let's give it a shot. It can't be any worse than what we're doing now, right?"

Feingold looked into Pete's eyes. Here was a man he had ruined financially. He had closed this man's business and even repossessed his home for a government auction to pay tax bills. Yet, here the man was, placing a hand of encouragement on his shoulder and smiling at him, offering uplifting words. If a man like Pete Fishers could be changed, then why couldn't . . . ?

"I . . . I'll just clear out my desk and . . ."

"No," said Jesus. "You don't need any of those items any longer. Let your secretary give them to other people. I want you to go with us now. Right now. Out the door. You can call your supervisor later and say that a letter of resignation is forthcoming. For now, however, I want you to leave with us. Be bold. Change your way of life today. We have other people to visit, other work to do. I want you with me every step of the way from now on."

Slowly, very slowly, Matthew Feingold nodded. After a moment, he stiffened his posture and pulled back his shoulders. He lifted his gaze. With an almost military about-face, he wheeled, jerked open the door, and stepped out of the room.

"There's a computer store down the street we're going to need to visit before it closes," he called back over his shoulder. "If I'm going to run an office, I'll need proper equipment and supplies."

Jesus and Pete hurried to catch up to him.

Section 3

How Jesus Revealed His Success Principles

My friend learned two of the procedures Jesus used to inspire and motivate workers: (1) sincere praise for a job well done, and (2) continuous restating of goals and objectives.

There is a great deal more, however, we can learn from Jesus about effective business management.

Employee Selections

Whereas at first glance it may have seemed the twelve men Jesus chose to be his disciples were not compatible, in time Jesus was able to form them into a working unit. The group benefited from their diversity.

Peter, Andrew, James, and John were sailors and fishermen. They knew how to use the land and sea to survive. Matthew and Judas were scholars. They could read, write, and handle money matters. Simon the Canaanite was a Zealot, someone who understood both politics and religion.

Although Jesus intended to give great new powers to his followers, he nevertheless saw the value of assembling a group with diverse backgrounds, experiences, and skills. He, himself, was both a tradesman (carpenter) and a scholar (rabbi, teacher). These diverse skills were shared and taught to one another during the years the disciples spent together. The Bible records several instances that bear this out.

After the crucifixion of Christ, for example, Peter grew restless and announced he was going fishing (John 21:3). James and John, the sons of Zebedee, went with him. There was nothing unusual about that, for they, too, were fishermen. But *with them* went Thomas and two other disciples. They went along *to help* with the fishing. They knew how to do it. They must have learned from Peter and the other fishermen.

Two lessons can be drawn from this: (1) Jesus believed in the value of having a diverse group of workers rather than pooling several carbon copies of one "standard" employee; and (2) Jesus encouraged cross-training. After three years, *all* could fish; *all* could read and write; *all* could travel and live off the land; and *all* could mingle with and gain acceptance by people of many different races, cultures, social strata, and nationalities. They taught each other and learned from each other and, in the process, they became a team.

Not everyone who applied for a position as a disciple was accepted by Jesus. He did not reject anyone for salvation, but he did make several people see they were not suitable for the discipleship job he had in mind. To one man, he explained there would be no income security and no job luxuries. To another, he explained there would be no emergency time off for family hardships or funerals. We have no record that either man followed Jesus. Thus, we see two other lessons: (1) Jesus believed

HOW JESUS REVEALED HIS SUCCESS PRINCIPLES

in carefully screening applicants, and (2) Jesus believed in having very specific job descriptions so workers would know what was expected of them.

In designing work assignments, Jesus did not use a seniority system. Instead, he issued duties and gave promotions in accordance with a person's capabilities, performance record, knowledge, and eagerness to achieve. Jesus had the ability to recognize hidden talents in people, and he had the patience to help people discover these talents in themselves and develop them to their fullest.

Jesus demonstrated this ability many times. He saw in the centurion (Matthew 8:13) a man of genuine leadership, discernment, and faith, and Jesus rewarded the man for his faith. Similarly, Matthew (Levi) was a man who was viewed by the Jews as someone who had "sold out" his people by becoming a tax collector for the Romans. Jesus, however, saw in Matthew a man who had the potential to be generous, open, and gracious. Jesus called Matthew away from his tax collecting. Matthew felt such joy and relief at this, he opened his home to the public and held a great party with plenty of food for lots of guests (Luke 5:29). Jesus had "read" Matthew correctly.

Probably the greatest example of discerning a person's potential is found in the life of Peter. To outsiders, this man was a roughshod, weather-beaten, uneducated, quick-tempered fisherman. To Jesus, however, he was a man of deep faith, rugged physical stamina, and natural leadership ability.

Jesus nurtured Peter's development in many areas. Some weeks after Jesus had ascended into heaven, Peter went boldly into the chambers of the priests and scribes and, there, against his opponents, he held his own in elocution, debating skills, and scriptural knowledge. His capabilities were so amazing, the

Bible says the elders and rulers "were astonished" at the fact that this man, whom they had considered to be "unschooled" and "ordinary," could now be so eloquent (Acts 4:13).

Part of the reason Jesus was able to make great leaders out of men like Peter and Matthew was because they were willing to strive for success. Too often we feel as though being success-oriented in life or business is not proper conduct for Christians. For a fact, it is failure that is not pleasing to the Lord.

Christ Endorsed Success

Have you ever wondered why some people ran away from success when it finally seemed so close to them? The Bible is filled with stories of such people. After God promised to make Moses a strong spokesman before Pharaoh, Moses shied away and let the gift of oratory go to Aaron. After the children of Israel reached the border of the Promised Land, they refused to cross over into it.

In truth, success can sometimes be so terrifying, we choose to flee from it. Avoid success? At first, it may seem ludicrous even to consider such a situation.

Upon closer examination, however, we find that the fear of success can take two forms: *pre-success anxiety*, in which a person is so fearful of succeeding that he or she does something to prevent it, and *success-status guilt*, in which a person who has achieved success cannot cope with it.

Jesus taught his followers to be successful in all they did. He, likewise, wants us to be committed to excellence, not content with mediocrity. Success, however, must be defined first by peace of mind. Jesus did not criticize Zacchaeus for being wealthy, but he showed him that his wealth would never give him the peace of mind he was seeking.

Similarly, Jesus did not criticize Peter and James for being fishermen, or Matthew for being a tax collector. He merely called them to something more challenging and demanding.

How about you? Do you have the talent and opportunity to be successful, yet perhaps lack the grit and determination to experience it? Let's take a moment to see why this may be so and how you can deal with it.

Whoa! to Success Woe

Some people are guilty of self-sabotage. It happens like this: just as a person is about to be promoted to manager or about to win a sales contest, he or she will suddenly become ill and will miss a week of work . . . or will purposely do something to aggravate the boss . . . or will even turn in a resignation.

It doesn't make sense, does it? Looking from the outside, perhaps not. But from the inside, it has a logic all its own. In research I did on this subject, I logged more than fifty so-called "good reasons" people had for thwarting their own success, including:

". . . and if I won the sales contest once, I'd be expected to win it again . . ."

". . . if I got promoted and my older sister didn't, she would be humiliated . . ."

". . . if I accepted the new position, I would have to transfer to Detroit, and I'm terrified of big cities . . ."

Such pre-success anxiety, whether real or imagined, exaggerated or accurately gauged, has kept scores of people in all walks of life from reaching their full potential.

Equally damaging is success-status guilt, which can often cause a person to topple herself or himself from a position of success after working years to get there. Sometimes, feelings of guilt or self-doubt arise when memories of the struggle to attain success prove embarrassing or confusing.

One man shared with me, "I became Outstanding Teacher of the State, but I can't forget that I broke my mother's heart when I didn't become a surgeon."

A woman told me, "In college I bragged I was going to become a famous portrait artist, but then I had a chance to become an ad designer with a major magazine. So, now I'm rolling in money, but I still feel like a failure."

Handling Success

There are several ways in which "fearful" Christians can learn how to cope with and accept success:

(1) If your success has been attained by the violation of any of God's laws, seek his forgiveness, correct your ways, and make restitution to those you've hurt or alienated. If you feel you cannot handle this alone, seek the help and guidance of a member of the clergy (Proverbs 15:16).

(2) Discard guilt over situations out of your control. If you were promoted because you were better qualified than your sister, it was your employer's choice, not yours. You cannot hold yourself responsible for your employer's needs or your sister's limitations. Just be gracious in your new status. Love conquers all.

(3) Remind yourself that as you mature, your goals will change. Maybe you now *prefer* to be an ad designer rather than a portrait painter. Fine! Both are legitimate and worthy occupations. It's *your* life, remember (Ecclesiastes 7:8).

HOW JESUS REVEALED HIS SUCCESS PRINCIPLES

(4) Be realistic about your accomplishments. It is better to be an outstanding teacher than a second-rate doctor, no matter what your mother thinks. (If she complains, tell her you wish she had married a billionaire since it would have made your life a lot easier, but you're willing to live and let live, if she is.)

(5) If the strain is too great, quit your job. Really. Let's face it, you aren't successful if you are miserable. Don't give yourself headaches and ulcers by compromising your principles. Get into a line of work you can be proud of. You made it to the top once; you can do it again.

(6) Keep in mind that some people are prone to jealousy. So, if someone tries to tell you that you don't deserve what you've earned, just consider the source. Maintain your confidence. You're on top because you worked for it.

Although the actual word *success* appears nowhere in the New International Version of the New Testament, the apostle John offers a perfect definition of success when he writes to Gaius, "Dear friend, I pray that you may enjoy good health and that all may go well with you, even as your soul is getting along well" (3 John 1:2).

What then is success?—a prosperous life, good health, and a righteous soul. In short, nothing to be terrified about.

The new wing of the building was still under construction, so Judas stepped carefully around hanging wires, stacks of lumber, temporary walls, and exposed joists. It was harder to navigate than a house of mirrors, but at last he turned a corner, ducked

underneath a low-hanging support beam, and located Jesus, who was in a squatting position on the ground.

"Here you are!"

Without turning around or rising, Jesus said, "Seek and you shall find. Watch your step, Judas. There are loose nails all over. If one goes through your hand or foot, it will be agonizing—trust me."

It was then that Judas noticed that Jesus was bent over one of the construction workers. Judas stepped cautiously forward to get a better look.

"What . . . what's going on here?"

"Gary here was sawing some boards, and he forgot to wear safety goggles," responded Jesus, still not looking at Judas. "A speck of wood got into his left eye, and I'm helping him get it out."

Judas shook his head in disbelief.

"*You're* what? You shouldn't be doing that. We have a company nurse available. A CEO doesn't get called away from the boardroom to remove a splinter from a common laborer. You have more important matters to focus on."

Gently, Jesus examined the man's eye. It was inflamed, dry, and puffy.

"Actually, I'm a common laborer," said Jesus in a low voice. "I can't tell you the number of times my brothers and I got wood chips in our eyes, under our fingernails, and in our hair. Our mother carefully removed them almost daily. That's where I learned how to handle things like this."

"We have a conference call set up with our distributors in L.A. and Atlanta in twenty minutes. Who would have the audacity to summon you down here to play nursemaid to a construction worker when we have much more important issues facing us?"

Jesus smiled. "In whose eyes?" He paused playfully. "Get it?"

Judas was in no mood for humor. "Can't you hurry it up?"

Once again Jesus examined the extended lower eyelid. Then, spitting into the dry lid, he pinched the splinter into the saliva pool and removed it with a tissue.

"Okay, Gary, your problem is solved. Get some eye drops from the nurse and rinse your eye every hour or so. Tomorrow, you'll be back to normal."

The worker lifted his hand to his face, then smiled. "Much obliged. It hurt like h—"

"No," Jesus quickly interrupted, "it didn't. But I know it was uncomfortable. Wear your protective eyewear from now on."

Gary nodded. "That's for sure. Thanks again."

"All right, all right, enough with the bedside manner," demanded Judas. "We've got to get back upstairs now. That call will be coming in, and we need to be there."

"Go ahead," said Jesus, still bent over the injured man. "I'll catch up with you."

"Please do so!" said Judas. "You're running out of time."

Judas whirled and smacked face-first into the low-hanging beam. Jesus and Gary heard the solid "whump" and turned in time to see Judas drop like a limp rag. He lay on the ground, completely unconscious.

"Whoa!" said Gary. "That had to hurt. Is he gonna be all right?"

Jesus arose. He looked at Judas for a few seconds.

"He'll survive. He's the hardest-headed guy on my staff, with a heart to match."

"You sure you don't need some help with him?"

Jesus shook his head. "No."

Gary got up and went to where Judas was lying and looked at him with his good eye. "Wow, look at the side of his face.

He'll have a shiner for a couple of weeks. Talk about being messed up!"

Jesus shrugged. "You don't know the half of it."

Gary looked around. "Maybe I should help you lift him and get him somewhere safe. If he comes to and is still dizzy, he could stumble into some of these loose wires and hang himself."

"Hmmm," said Jesus, looking at the fallen body. "Of course we wouldn't want something like that to happen. Okay, come on, let's get him up to the boardroom." He reached to lift Judas by the shoulders. "At least he'll be present for the conference call he was so worried about."

Section 4

JESUS ON CLOSING A SALE

There's an adage that says, "Everybody lives by selling something." If you work for a living, that's true of you. If you aren't selling a product, then you're selling a service.

I've spent most of my life as a salesman. When I was a teenager, I taught guitar lessons at a small music store, and I earned commissions on the instruments I sold to my students. During college, I worked part-time for my dad's optical company, and I sold eyedrops, frames, cases, and examining equipment to doctors.

As a writer, I've sold articles to magazines and book manuscripts to publishers. As a workshop director, I've even sold "selling," in that I've been hired to teach seminars on sales techniques at numerous marketing conferences and conventions. Selling helps me survive in the secular world. It may surprise you to learn, however, that it also has a place in my religious life.

Frequently, when I'm asked by people to help them learn how to be more effective witnesses for Jesus Christ, I very often say that the same five basic steps used in selling a product or service can be used just as effectively in winning someone to the Lord. To prove it, let me review those five steps with you:

Step One: *Believe in the product yourself.* I would not buy an American-built car from a salesperson who drove a foreign sports car. My logic would be, "If this guy is telling me I'm buying the best car on the road, why isn't *he* driving one?" Similarly, I wouldn't buy a baby alligator from a woman with two missing fingers on her right hand, no matter how much she tried to tell me it made a lovable pet. The credibility factor just wouldn't be there.

There's a parallel to this in the religious world. No one is going to be excited about developing a Spirit-filled life if the person telling him or her about it displays no Christian virtues or disciplines. If, however, an unbeliever sees someone enjoying a walk with God through prayer, Bible reading, church attendance, and Christian fellowship, that person will sense sincerity in the one who witnesses to him or her. The witness will have true credibility.

Jesus explained this same sales tip in Matthew 5:16 when he said, "Let your light shine before others, that they may see your good deeds and glorify your Father in heaven."

Step Two: *Know the product thoroughly.* There's nothing worse than dealing with a salesperson who has to keep flipping through the pages of an instruction manual each time you ask a question. Conversely, nothing instills confidence more than dealing with a knowledgeable salesperson.

I once went with a friend to shop for an exercise bike. The saleswoman could not be stumped by any question we threw at her. She knew everything from the cost of a replacement handlebar to the number of wheel revolutions at twenty-five miles per hour. When she made a recommendation about what bike my friend needed, he took her advice. She was a proven expert. And she made the sale.

What about you? Your product manual is the Bible. How well do you know it? If someone asks you a question about doctrine, can you quote verses from memory or at least know where to turn immediately for the appropriate passages? Having to leaf through an index and then run a cross-reference in a concordance makes it appear you have no more familiarity with the Scriptures than a nonbeliever. It doesn't inspire confidence. It raises doubts that you know what you are talking about.

Paul admonished us to remember "the words the Lord Jesus himself said" (Acts 20:35) and to "direct the affairs of the church well" (1 Timothy 5:17). It's good sales training.

Step Three: *Master more than one sales approach.* In selling, the key to success is in customizing the sales technique to the behavior of the customer. For some people who like to talk, the "Q & A" approach is best: the salesperson asks questions and uses the customers' answers to draw them into the sale. For people who hate to talk, a "demonstration" is more effective: customers get to try out the product for themselves and, thereby, sell themselves on it. For other people, a "comparison/contrast" approach is best: the superior abilities of the new product are used to overshadow the less-capable product the customer is currently using.

Competent salespeople develop more than a dozen procedures to attract a customer's attention to a product. Likewise, an effective soul winner will realize not all lost people can be won to the Lord through direct witnessing. For some people, the approach must be through "friendship evangelism," wherein you offer to form a carpool with a new neighbor or you ask someone over to dinner several times. After a time of developing a friendship, you can share your love of Jesus with your friend.

Other people need "side-door evangelism." They won't accept an offer to go to church with you on Sunday, but they *will* take part in your Tuesday-night church softball league. As you pray before the start of a game, show good attitudes on the field (win or lose), and welcome the newcomer as a teammate, he or she will become more open to a sharing of God's Word.

Jesus used many different techniques in sharing the Good News. He preached to crowds of thousands; he led his disciples in small-group discussions; he counseled Nicodemus one-on-one; he debated the scribes; he discussed Scripture with the elders; he used comparison/contrast techniques with the people who were going to stone the adulteress; he offered object lessons and parables to the uneducated masses. Whatever the situation called for, Jesus was able to use the appropriate delivery. We would do well to emulate his versatility.

Step Four: *Stress quality*. People will pay top dollar for high quality. A regular letter going by US postal service from Baltimore to San Diego will arrive in five days for under a dollar. FedEx will cost a few dollars, but it will arrive in two days. A text message will cost much more for the technology, but it will arrive in two seconds. Quality service carries a steep price, but its benefits are great.

Likewise, the Christian life exacts a high price: its disciplines are inflexible, its walk is sometimes lonely, and its rewards are frequently not received this side of heaven. Nevertheless, the quality of the Christian life makes the price seem inconsequential. Having the ability to *rest* in Jesus whenever tired, to *trust* in God even as humankind's strategies fail, and to *rejoice* in all circumstances because the Lord never changes, provides a quality of life no unredeemed person can experience.

Just living by God's Word is real "success" (Joshua 1:8). The quality of our souls is like the highest quality gold that has had all its impurities refined out (Revelation 3:18). When you talk to others about your life as a Christian, stress this quality.

Step Five: *Offer a guarantee.* Reputable places of business will guarantee the capability and durability of their goods and services. Trade names such as Kraft, Schwinn, RCA, Microsoft, Steinway, Mazda, Nabisco, and many others have prospered for many years by guaranteeing the excellence of their products.

Christianity, too, provides many guarantees: a life of peace (Romans 5:1); God's boundless love (2 Timothy 2:9); fellowship with other believers (Acts 2:42); and a joint inheritance of God's kingdom and glory (Romans 8:17). These are but a few of the many *guaranteed* benefits provided by a Spirit-filled life. And how solid are the guarantees? Well . . . we have God's *Word* (the Bible) on it!

The Best Product

A representative of the Rolls-Royce automotive firm was once asked why his company never ran a year-end sale or a model changeover sale or *any kind* of sale. "There's no need," he responded. "When you have a product that offers as much as our product offers, it's all we can do to keep up with demand."

If such a statement can be made of a car, imagine what can be said of the Christian life. Are you sold on it? If so, you've just met the requirements of Step One in the process of selling it to someone else.

Jesus was seated behind his desk in his office when a burly security officer entered.

"We found our thief," the man announced. He pulled a woman forward and pushed her into a leather chair.

The man's partner, a female carrying a clipboard and wearing the blue uniform shirt of their subcontracted company, appeared in the room and nodded agreement.

"We've got surveillance tape of her going into the supply closet," she explained, as she scanned notes on her clipboard. "We grabbed her when she came out and found a box of pens, box of pencils, box of paper clips, six batteries, and five pads of paper in her big purse. We searched her locker and found a small stash of similar items that have been coming up missing. No doubt about it, she's the sneak thief who's been pilfering from the company for the past month. We've got her."

Jesus looked at the woman, but she would not lift her eyes to him. He remained at his desk, saying nothing. The room was silent for a moment, then suddenly three more employees arrived.

"I just got word that Security nailed our thief," said Judas. "This her? Good job. Anyone call the city cops yet?"

"No, sir," said the male security guard. "Thought we should bring her here to the top brass first." He nodded toward another new arrival, Tom Scarsdale, head of internal plant security. "That what you want, Mr. Scarsdale? Should I call the city police? I've got them on speed dial." He held up his cell phone.

"Who is she?" asked Tom. "I thought I knew most of our people."

"A recent hire," said Johnny Brothers, director of training, moving to the center of the room. "Mary Wilder. Been here about two months. I hired her to work in quality control. She inspects our rockers, baby cribs, and high chairs for any deficiencies before we ship 'em out. Got a good eye, too. Been a good employee. Until now, I mean. Never late, never absent, always conscientious on the job. Seemed like an ideal worker." He turned toward Jesus. "Sorry, Boss. Appears I hired a bad apple."

Jesus opened a drawer, took out a yellow pad of paper and a felt-tip pen. He said nothing, but began to jot some notes on the pad.

"Do you have anything to say for yourself?" Tom asked the woman. "Theft is a serious crime, no matter what amount was stolen. Didn't you realize we'd catch you sooner or later?"

Without lifting her head, the woman said, "I was going to pay it back . . . replace it all. I really was." She wiped tears from her eyes. "I'm a single mother. My kids . . . they need school supplies. I never seem to have enough money. Rent . . . food . . . even with riding public transportation and buying used clothes, I'm always short. I didn't mean any harm. Just a few items . . . for a few weeks, until I got my first raise. Then I was going to . . ."

"You think you're above the law?" demanded Judas. "The rules don't apply to you, is that it? Well, think again. We've got a business to run here. Our profit margin is razor thin as it is. We let you get away with taking paper clips today, it'll be a computer or a lathe machine next week."

A few snickers were heard in the room.

"Don't exaggerate," cautioned Tom. "She's not Public Enemy Number One. Let's dock her pay for all the stolen items, fire her, and move on."

Judas shook his head. "Sure, and then word gets out that there's no retribution for theft in the company. What kind of message does that send to the other employees? No! I say we make an example of her. I know I'm right about this." He looked sideways at where Jesus still sat, continuing to jot notes on the pad before him, but saying nothing.

"Please!" said Mary, suddenly. "I need this job. I'm sorry. I'll repay everything, yes. And I'll never do anything like this again. I give you my word."

"Oh, golly-gee, that's certainly reassuring," said Judas with a sneer. "You steal from us for the past month every chance you get, and now you offer us your 'word' that you can be trusted. Sorry, no deal, Lady. 'Burn me once' is my motto." He did an about-face. "What're you waiting for, Tom? Call the city police, show them the evidence, and press charges against her. We've got other work we all need to get back to."

"I doubt it's that simple," said Tom.

"You doubt a lot of things," countered Judas. "For once, take a stand. Do your job!"

"I *am* doing my job," Tom responded, fighting to stay in control. "For now, this is still an internal matter. This woman made a mistake. A bad one. I'm not saying we should turn a blind eye to what she did. But I can't see where putting a single mom behind bars is the best resolution of this incident. Once we call in the local authorities, we'll forfeit our jurisdiction. Let's think this through a little more."

Judas raised and lowered his hands. "What's with you?" he demanded. "You're the head of plant security. You caught her red-handed. For two cents, I'd turn her in myself."

"You'd want more than that," said Jesus, catching everyone off guard. He'd been so quiet, they had almost forgotten why they'd come to his office in the first place. Now, all turned and gave him their full attention.

JESUS ON CLOSING A SALE

Jesus rose from his desk and came around in front of it, holding the pad of paper in his right hand. "You're all concerned that what this woman has done has caused harm to the company," he said flatly. "You're worried it may cause a ripple effect. If others mimic her actions, we'll soon be left with nothing but bare walls, right?"

"Stealing is wrong," interjected Judas. "I'm sure you won't deny that."

Jesus smiled wistfully, almost as though the comment had amused him. "No, I won't argue that. Not for a moment."

He took a few steps until he was standing before the female security officer. He glanced down at the notes on his writing pad and said, "If someone is habitually fifteen or twenty minutes late for work, yet that person always draws full pay, that is a form of theft, isn't it?"

He then looked at the male security officer and added, "And, if someone falsely logged that delinquent person into work 'on time,' that would be deception, and fraud, and complicity in an illegal act, wouldn't it?"

He took a short sidestep until he was in front of John Brothers, then glanced at his notepad once more. "And, if someone occasionally used a company vehicle for personal errands, that would constitute a form of stealing, no doubt."

Turning to Tom Scarsdale he added, "Likewise, if someone didn't show up for mandatory committee meetings or was lax in doing regular checks of safety measures throughout the building, such actions would be thefts of time."

He next looked Judas directly in the face and said, "And, if someone padded an expense account by ten or twelve dollars per week, that would be an even worse theft than what Mary here has done."

Jesus eased back behind his desk and sat. As he did so, he turned the notepad face down on his desk. Everyone stared hard at it, but no one said a word.

"Yes," said Jesus, "I'm definitely against stealing. In any form, by any person." He paused a moment to allow his words to register. "But I'm also aware that people don't always think of themselves as thieves, even when they're in the act of stealing. Like Mary, here, they justify their actions, or make excuses, or promise themselves they'll be better tomorrow."

Almost dramatically, he turned the notepad over and tore off the top three sheets that contained all the notes he had been writing since everyone had entered his office. He extended his arm to the left and fed the pages into a paper shredder near his desk. The whirring noise was virtually music to the ears of every person in the room.

"Sometimes, maybe, we just need to hope people actually will be able to curb their bad habits and misguided behaviors," said Jesus, now leaning forward with his elbows on his desk. "It may not always be possible, but perhaps if we show folks some mercy, some understanding, some trust, they won't go on disappointing us. What do you think? Am I wrong in feeling this way?"

The room remained quiet, no one daring to voice a contrary opinion. Jesus waited a long time, then said, "Well, then, it seems we're in agreement. So, we now need to determine what to do about our co-worker here."

He looked at the security workers and asked, "Are you willing to forgive Mary, if she promises to repay what she's stolen and never do it again?"

Neither guard could actually speak, but they nodded their assent.

JESUS ON CLOSING A SALE

"Good. Very good." Jesus shifted his gaze and asked, "Johnny? Tom? Would you fellows be willing to work out some kind of internal company probation for Mary?"

The two men glanced quickly at each other, reading one another's mind. "Uh, yes, sir," they both said in low voices, almost simultaneously.

"I appreciate that," said Jesus. Finally, he looked at Judas, who, unlike the others was not standing in a slump-shouldered, humbled stance. Instead, his eyes showed anger, as though he had been personally insulted and publicly humiliated. His defiance and seething rage were evident, although he bit his lip and reined in his emotions.

"And can I count on you to give Mary one more chance to redeem herself, Judas?"

For an instant the two men stood in a face-off. The others could tell that Judas did not agree with such a benevolent resolution of this situation, that he wanted Mary to serve as an example of what harsh and strict management was all about. However, as Jesus stayed in calm control of the circumstances, Judas recognized he'd been out-voted, out-maneuvered, and out-classed in this instance. He would have to bide his time, choosing another day and venue to make his move to assert his authority.

"As you wish," Judas responded at last, biting off each word. With that, he pushed his way through the others and made his exit.

Not knowing what else to say or do, the other four employees filed silently out of the office.

"You're not going to press charges?" asked Mary, looking at Jesus in genuine amazement.

"I never intended to have you arrested," answered Jesus. "Your accusers were the people who brought you in here. Where are they now?"

Mary looked around the empty office and then at the open door. "They're gone," she said. "They've gone back to work."

"Then I suggest you go back to work, too," said Jesus.

"But . . . I mean . . . I don't know what to . . . ."

"Just say you won't steal from us again," said Jesus. "That's all that's needed. But mean what you say."

Mary nodded. "Yes, sir. I'm so grateful. You're so kind. I won't disappoint you. Never. I promise." She rose from her chair. "When they brought me in here, I thought that . . . I assumed . . . ."

"Don't dwell on that, Mary," said Jesus. "Just go back to work and show everyone you're not the same person. I have faith in you."

Tears welled up anew in Mary's eyes. "Thank you," she said very softly. "That means a lot to me. I needed to hear that. More than you'll ever know."

Jesus smiled kindly. "Oh, I do know," he assured her. "Trust me, I do *know*."

Section 5

JESUS ON QUALITY CONTROL

We know from studying the life of Jesus that he was a perfectionist. Although he was forgiving of others who failed in their work, he, himself, was perfect in all things. This provides an ideal for us to try to emulate.

Biblical references to quality control in work are found in both the Old and New Testaments.

The men who were commissioned by young King Josiah to repair the Lord's temple had a tremendous challenge facing them. Without the aid of modern power tools, cranes, buzz saws, or forklifts, they had to build new stone walls, lay a new wooden floor, and then do all new interior decorating. The Bible summarized their job performance by noting, "The workers labored faithfully" (2 Chronicles 34:12).

How about the work you are engaged in? Do the qualities of your Christian tenets—honesty, excellence, diligence, dependability—show themselves in your performance? If they do not, you are not only shaming yourself, but you are also casting Christianity itself in a bad light.

We have been reared under a dangerous belief: "To err is human; to forgive, divine." In reality, we should believe that "to err is inhumane" (for what right have we to foist shoddy workmanship upon others?) and "to forgive, unfortunate" (since we shouldn't be making errors in the first place).

The emphasis in American business today is upon "zero defects." Companies do not want to detect errors; they want to prevent them from occurring in the first place. Shouldn't Christians desire to be equally diligent in a quest for excellent service?

I made this point not long ago in a luncheon speech I gave before a group of Christian business leaders. Later, one man confronted me and said, "Only Christ was perfect. You can't expect people to do flawless work all the time. Even my union allows for a 10 percent margin of error. You should be more tolerant."

"What you're saying may be acceptable in some cases," I responded. "However, what if everyone felt the same way you do? That would mean surgeons could accidentally kill one patient in ten. It would mean wrecking crews could knock down the wrong house on every tenth job. It would mean parachute packers could allow ten soldiers to plunge to their deaths out of every one hundred who jumped from an airplane. Do you think we should be more tolerant of that?"

The man paused, then grimaced and said, "Uh, not if I'm the one being operated on or jumping from the plane. I see your point."

Everything we do should be done to the glory of God, for the Bible says, "Commit to the Lord whatever you do" (Proverbs 16:3). Christ was committed to completing his entire task. Can we be any less diligent?

JESUS ON QUALITY CONTROL

Why Quality Slips

There are five major reasons for poor quality work. You should be aware of them, lest you fall victim to them:

(1) *A Lack of Attention.* Workers who are too bored, too restless, or too tired prove to be shoddy performers. To avoid this, we need to get adequate rest, vary our daily routines, and sometimes just schedule a time to "get away from it all."

(2) *A Lack of Drive.* Workers who are physically ill or under great mental or emotional stress will not have the concentration and commitment needed to do a job well. It is better to stay home and recover from a cold, or travel to another city to be near a loved one who is undergoing an operation, than to drag ourselves into work knowing that the body and mind are not willing to perform.

(3) *A Poor Attitude.* Workers who are willing to accept mediocrity as a standard are going to cause as many problems as they solve. The "middle" is as close to rock bottom as it is to the top. Just as Christ cannot tolerate a lukewarm church (Revelation 3:16), he cannot take pride in a nonchalant worker. As Christian workers, we must set high standards for ourselves.

(4) *A Refusal to Accept Instruction.* Workers who are too proud, too bossy, too busy, or too afraid to show a weakness will not allow themselves to be taught new and better ways to work. Soon, their outdated work habits become a detriment to the overall work effort. Rather, we should be eager to attend seminars, read helpful books and magazines, and ask for advice and

suggestions on ways to improve our work. We should always be looking for a better way.

(5) *A Lack of Awareness.* Some workers believe that quality control relates only to someone who sits on an assembly line and removes any defective products that may come by. This is naive. Quality control should apply to service as well as products. We should strive to be excellent in everything we commit ourselves to. This especially applies to our service to God (2 Timothy 2:15).

In Shakespeare's classic play *Julius Caesar,* Brutus tries to blame the failure of the rebellion against Caesar on the stars and on fate and on happenstance. His co-conspirator Cassius knows better, however. He accepts his failure and tells his companion, "The fault, dear Brutus, is not in our stars, but in ourselves."

We need to face that same fact. If our work is not of high quality, the fault is "in ourselves."

Getting the Job Done

A word of caution is needed here. Whereas we should strive for quality and excellence in all we do, we do not want to hide behind a veil of perfectionism as an excuse for never completing a project. Indeed, in business, in addition to quality, productivity is an essential element in the success of an operation. And Jesus had a great deal to say about productivity, job completion, and self-motivation. Recently, after I gave a one-hour motivational speech at a gathering of Sunday school teachers and other church workers, I was approached by a lady who told me coldly, "You need to learn that God is not keeping score

JESUS ON QUALITY CONTROL

regarding our accomplishments here on Earth. My heart is pure and my eyes are on Christ. That's what really matters, sir!"

I smiled, nodded my agreement, and said, "Indeed—for *your* life. But what about your next-door neighbor and your dentist and your beautician? Are *their* hearts pure and are *their* eyes on Christ? If not, I guarantee you that your salvation is not going to save them. It is your witnessing that is going to make a difference. Don't equate confidence about your own spiritual situation with behavior that is glorifying to God. You are only halfway successful; you've found salvation for yourself, but now you must find it for others. Do some work!"

Noted management specialist Philip B. Crosby once stated, "Not failing is not the same as succeeding." That statement holds a great truth. It could be phrased another way: "There is no status quo. You are either moving ahead, or you are losing ground."

The same thing is true of the Christian life. There is no such thing as success in general—there is only success at something. Whatever your particular talent is, it should be directed toward some sort of ministry or service. If you are moving closer to achieving that goal, you are successful. If you are *not* advancing toward the goal—or, far worse, if you are drifting away from it—you are failing.

Now note—I did not say that your goal had to be something that turned the world upside down. All I said was that you should *have* a goal, and you should be moving toward achieving it. God will be pleased with even the smallest efforts, if they are made with the sincerest attitude of sacrifice or devotion. When the widow gave her last bit of flour and olive oil to a prophet, and a different widow donated two very small copper coins to the temple treasury, both efforts were considered monumental deeds in God's eyes, though by human standards they were insignificant contributions.

God does not want the service of a "blowhard." I once knew a man who boasted that after he received his holiday bonus, he was going to buy all new choir robes for the church. He also promised that once his work schedule was changed to second shift, he would help the pastor make calls on the needy. He talked of great things, but he never got around to doing any of them. Meanwhile, an elderly lady in our church worked faithfully as a nursery helper every Wednesday night and every Sunday morning. Her small work efforts were of far greater value than the unachieved big plans of the talkative man.

Ecclesiastes 5:3-4 explains, "A dream [goal] comes when there are many cares [is much work], and many words mark the speech of a fool. When you make a vow to God, do not delay to fulfill it. He has no pleasure in fools; fulfill your vow."

God is pleased by successful workers. When David raised up a great army and went out to reclaim the land of Israel (his work), God gave him victory. When Solomon built the great temple (his work), God blessed it. When Joshua attacked the inhabitants of Canaan (his work), God gave him land. When Nehemiah developed a plan to rebuild the walls of Jerusalem (his work), God protected the workers and provided the materials.

Conversely, God "takes no pleasure in fools" who neglect to do the work he has called them to. As we noted earlier, when Moses was too meek to speak before Pharaoh, God took the gift of oratory away and gave it to Moses' brother Aaron. When Jonah ran from the assignment to preach in Nineveh, God caused a huge fish to swallow him and then vomit him on a seashore. When John Mark could not maintain the pace of aggressive evangelism that Paul was setting, Paul dismissed him from the work and sent him home.

Fortunately, the grace of God allows each of us to make "comebacks," to recover from times of failure and weakness. When Moses worked with Aaron, the brothers were able to secure the release of the Israelites from Egypt and lead them to the Promised Land. After the fish vomited Jonah onto dry land, Jonah was able to redirect his path toward God's original goal for him and, thereby, bring revival to the people of Nineveh. John Mark was sent home, yet he later apparently was reconciled with Paul, for we read in Colossians 4:10, "My fellow prisoner Aristarchus sends you his greetings, as does Mark, the cousin of Barnabas," and in 2 Timothy 4:11, "Only Luke is with me. Get Mark and bring him with you, because he is helpful to me in my ministry."

Even though grace is available when we fail, God's people and his churches are not honoring him when they are complacent and neutral. God gave a message to the church at Laodicea that needs to be heeded by all churches and all Christians: "I know your deeds, that you are neither cold nor hot. I wish you were either one or the other! So, because you are lukewarm—neither hot nor cold—I am about to spit you out of my mouth" (Revelation 3:15–16). It is amazing how similar this sounds to Crosby's admonition that not failing is not the same as succeeding. God's will is for us to *succeed* at a God-honoring work.

Jesus succeeded in all he set out to accomplish here on Earth. Not only that, but he spent time teaching his followers that they, too, should succeed at some work for God the Father. It is not enough to warm a pew on Sunday mornings. There is work to do.

Jesus explained it once with a little story (Luke 13:6–9). A man owned a lovely orchard that gave him many delicious fruits to eat and sell. Amidst the orchard, however, was one large tree that had many branches, many lush green leaves and many deep and strong roots, yet this tree never produced any fruit. The landowner had been patient with the tree for three growing seasons, but in none of those years did it yield figs.

Finally, the landowner told his head gardener to chop down the tree, clear out the roots, and plant a new tree on that spot so that eventually there would be fruit coming from that section of the orchard. The head gardener understood his employer's frustration, but he suggested an alternate plan. He asked that he be allowed to irrigate the land around the tree so more water could get to the roots, and that he be allowed to fertilize the soil so nutrients could get into the tree. He promised his employer that if this did not succeed in helping the tree bear fruit then, indeed, the tree would be chopped down.

We should take this as a warning. If we are a large but unproductive tree planted in one of God's vineyards (a church, a Christian youth group, an evangelistic outreach), we are not in a neutral position—we are actually taking up room where someone more productive could be serving and ministering. God the Father, as the landowner, has the option of removing us and eliminating the hindrance we are causing. Christ, as the patient gardener, wants to give us yet another chance. He wants to encourage us to sink our roots into God's Word and become productive for his ministry. However, if we will not heed his suggestions and encouragements, then he may determine that it is best for us to be removed from our orchard of ministry.

How about you? Are you succeeding at anything? Sooner or later harvest time will come. When it does, what will you show—abundance or barrenness? It has to be one or the other, because not failing is not the same as succeeding.

Jesus, Pete, and Matt were only a block away from their favorite noontime café when a stranger stepped onto the sidewalk, blocking their way.

"Excuse me a moment," he said, holding out a business card toward Jesus. "I was wondering if I could have five minutes of your time."

Pete reached over and snatched the business card from the man's hand. Aloud he read, "Richard Youngman, CEO, Youngman Imports–Exports." He looked at Matt, who shook his head. "We never heard of ya," Pete said to the stranger. "Maybe some other time. Right now, I got an appointment with a plate of catfish."

"Please, sir, just five minutes," the man repeated, looking directly at Jesus.

Jesus smiled. "I'll turn no one away who seeks me. Come on. Join us for lunch."

The stranger fell in line and walked with the other three. He was in his early 30s, wearing expensive loafers, tailored slacks, a monogrammed dress shirt, silk tie, and a smartly cut sport coat. In one hand he carried a thin briefcase made of hand-tooled leather.

When they arrived at Gino's Café, there was a hand-scrawled sign on the door reading, "Closed—Deliveries Never Arrived."

"Hey! What's with this?" Pete demanded. "I'm ready to chow down, and this place is closed? No way!"

Jesus peered through the glass of the front door and spotted the owner inside. He knocked on the window and motioned for

Gino to come forward. The owner slowly made his way to the front and unlocked the door.

"Sorry, boys, no fish today," he said through the half-opened door. "My delivery man never showed up. Come back tomorrow, okay?"

"You haven't got enough for just the three of us?" Pete implored.

"Four," chimed in the stranger.

Gino lifted his palms in a sign of resignation. "It's the bridge into town. An accident occurred this morning, and it shut down all lanes. My bread truck didn't arrive either. I'm down to the few leftovers that weren't used yesterday. Couple of loaves of bread and a few fish still in the freezer."

Jesus eased his way inside. "Let me take a look, Gino. I've been known to make food stretch when necessary."

"See for yourself, my friend," said Gino, pointing to his kitchen. "My cooks and waitresses are getting ready to leave. We've got nothing to do today."

Jesus motioned to Matt, Pete, and Richard to take seats at one of the empty tables. He went to the back alone and pushed through the swinging metal doors. He was impressed with the cleanliness of the kitchen. The stainless steel counters were spotless. The stoves and ranges were free of grease splatters. The utensils were clean and hanging in order.

Gino came in behind Jesus.

"This place is immaculate," said Jesus.

Gino nodded. "Well, you know what they say: 'Cleanliness is next . . .'"

"Yes," interrupted Jesus. "I have heard that." He walked to the freezer door and opened it and peered in. "Would you be interested in building your business, Gino?"

"Naturally," said Gino. "But today . . . no food."

JESUS ON QUALITY CONTROL

"I'll see to it that you have plenty of fish and plenty of loaves of bread," promised Jesus, "if, in return, you and your staff will give away meals all day today. No charge. Invite hundreds of people in for fish dinners. Serve them, but don't charge them. It'll be a great way to expose your business to people who've never eaten here. And, as an added bonus, I'll see to it that you have enough food left over to run your business the rest of the week without having to place new orders."

Gino looked confused. "But the bridge . . ."

"I have other sources. Do we have a deal?"

Gino lifted one hand. "Wait, please. I'll go talk to my employees." He turned and disappeared through the swinging doors. After he left, Jesus bowed his head for a moment.

Five minutes later Gino came back into the kitchen, his two short-order cooks following him. "Okay. Somehow, if you can get us the fish and bread, we'll do the cooking and serving."

Jesus pointed a finger toward the freezers. "The first shipment arrived while you were out there talking. Get started."

Gino smirked. "What are you talking about? I didn't hear any trucks. Besides, I've only been gone a couple of minutes."

"See for yourself."

Hesitantly, Gino walked to one of the freezers and opened the door. He flinched in shock. "Holy cow!"

"No," said Jesus, sighing. "And after a few thousand years, I'm really getting tired of that expression." He turned away. "You have your food, now start distributing the meals. Start by bringing my friends and me some platters."

"All this fish!" said Gino, pulling his chef's hat off and running his fingers through his hair. "It's a miracle. How can it be? It's . . . it's a miracle. Holy mackerel!"

Jesus was privately amused. "Indeed."

JESUS IN THE 9 TO 5

"So, what is it you wanted to see us about?" Matt Feingold asked the stranger now sharing lunch with them.

Looking at Jesus, the young man asked, "In the kitchen . . . how . . . how did you . . . how were you able . . . ?"

"Stay focused," said Matt. "You asked for five minutes. You're getting it. What did you want?"

The man shook his head as if to clear it. "Uh . . . I'm Richard Youngman," he said.

"Yeah, I read your card," said Pete, speaking with his mouth full. "Remember?"

"I . . . I've heard of the success you've had in making and marketing your furniture. I have contacts. Lot of contacts worldwide. Europe, South America, Southeast Asia, India, China—I ship and sell products all over the globe for companies. I could triple your output, and make a lot of money for you."

The three men gave small smiles to each other. "What makes you think we want to work three times harder than we're already working?" asked Pete.

"No, no, not that," said Youngman. "We could outsource most of the work, using cheaper labor overseas. All they'd need would be your blueprints or schematics or designs—whatever you use in the furniture business—and they could make copies and ship products directly. Once everything was in place, you'd just have to collect your share of the profits."

"And you could set all this up for us?" asked Matt.

"I could. I've done it for nearly a dozen other companies thus far."

"And your cut would be . . . ?"

JESUS ON QUALITY CONTROL

"A modest upfront fee and then a small continuing percentage of all future sales. All very fair, I assure you."

"Fair to whom?" asked Jesus in a low and steady voice.

"Why, to everyone," said Youngman. "To you, as CEO . . . to your stockholders, if you ever go public . . . to the people who would buy your furniture at even lower prices in the future. There's no downside anywhere."

"Think the underpaid overseas laborers would consider it fair?" asked Jesus.

"Most of them are starving," said Youngman. "They need work of any kind. We'd be doing them a favor. Besides, they can get along on a lot less than we do in America. They're used to it."

Matt said, "The poor will always be with us."

Jesus raised an eyebrow. "Nice line," he said. "I couldn't have said it better myself."

"Doesn't make it right, though," said Pete, biting off an endcrust of bread. "I've been poor. I know about that. Yeah, you work . . . take whatever you can get. But it don't mean you're happy 'bout it. Don't mean you're proud of what you're doin'."

Youngman pushed his plate aside and rested his elbows on the table so he could gesture with his hands as he made his case. "Look," he began, feigning earnestness, "I've read about you guys, all about your company. You hire street people and give them training. You hire druggies and help them stay clean. You hire minorities and treat them as equals. I've done my research. I know all about your plant, your workers, your modus operandi."

"Wow!" said Pete. "The guy speaks French. Impressive."

"I can identify with what you're doing," continued Youngman, not appreciating interruptions. "You're turning a solid *profit while also helping to restore the community. What could be nobler than that?"*

"So, you're into being a noble man, is that it?" asked Jesus.

Youngman smiled. "Certainly. I want to throw in with you guys. Become one of you. Focus on the same goals . . . share the same noble ambitions . . ."

". . . take a cut of the annual profits," said Matt, removing his eyeglasses to clean them with one of the paper napkins.

Youngman paused, then lifted one shoulder. "Well, sure, there's always that. But of greater importance would be to further the good work you men have already started. I'd just be helping you to spread it globally."

"Sounds great," said Jesus, smiling warmly.

"It does?" said Pete. "Maybe I missed something."

Youngman reached to the floor and lifted his fancy briefcase into his lap. He opened it and began extracting some papers. "So, we have a deal then?"

"Oh, you won't need any contracts," said Jesus. "We work mostly on an honor system. I give the directives, and you honor them."

Youngman looked slightly confused. "Well, yes . . . but I'm sure you'll agree that a few ground rules would be in order."

Jesus nodded. "Tell you what. Since you're so eager to help those poor people overseas find a better way of life, I'd like you to put your money—and it will be your money—where your mouth is. Matt, here, is our financial officer. I'd like you to sign over all your stocks, bonds, certificates of deposit, and bank accounts to an overseas charity already being funded by our company. Matt will see to the final transfers for you. Once that's all accomplished, you can step in as our new Overseas Operations Manager."

JESUS ON QUALITY CONTROL

Youngman sat frozen, utterly perplexed. Then, slowly, he began to smile. "It's a joke, right? I mean, you're kidding me, right?"

Pete lifted his coffee cup, took a sip, then lowered it. "He ain't much into sayin' what he don't mean, partner. I'm pretty sure he's serious."

Youngman shook his head slightly. "But, you have no idea how much money you're talking about here."

"Wanna bet?" said Pete. "Portfolios ain't no big deal for him. You should see him do this 'hairs on your head' thing. Cracks me up every time."

Youngman stared wide-eyed directly at Jesus. "You honestly expect me to sell everything I own, give it to some charity, and then report to work for you as some kind of salaried worker?"

"Some kind," confirmed Jesus.

The young executive pushed back his chair and rose. "I've worked hard for what I have."

Matt looked up at him. "Then enjoy it . . . if you can. I've been down that road. You came here today because you're looking for something, Richard. And you found it, but now you don't have the guts to grab it. And I'm not berating you, son. Lord knows, it's a hard decision to make."

He barely heard Jesus mumble, "Yes, I do. I do know."

"You're asking too much," said Youngman. "You want me to sell my soul to your business, and I'm not about to do that."

"Don't sell it," said Jesus, with genuine compassion. "Redeem it."

Richard Youngman looked from Jesus to Matt to Pete and then to Jesus again. A surprisingly pained look formed on his face. For a second, it seemed as though he might change his mind, or at least might say something else. But, no, in the end, he just turned from the table and walked resolutely out the door.

No one spoke. After a moment, Gino came to the table.

"Great lunch crowd, boys. Any dessert?"

Pete reached for a toothpick and stuck it between his teeth. "Can't eat another bite, Gino." He looked around the diner. "But looks like ya still got plenty of leftovers. Pack up some to-go bags. We'll take 'em with us for the boys on the night shift."

"You got it," said Gino. He smiled broadly. "You're never gonna guess how many people we served today."

Jesus said, "It was exactly . . ."

"Oh, stop!" interjected Matt.

Section 6

Jesus on Setting and Reaching Goals

As a motivational speaker, I am very interested in what drives people. I'm curious as to why individuals buy or sell, work or rest, save or spend, advance or retreat, build or tear down.

I've spent years conducting and accumulating research related to what drives a person to strive for something great, never resting until a goal is reached. I've studied a wide range of data on what separates winners from losers. In all my studies, no lessons related to personal achievement have impressed me more than those I have drawn from the account of the Magi.

We first can note that the Wise Men were *focused on one star*, not fifteen or twenty. They were unified, organized, and headed in the same direction. Many of today's problems could be solved if families, churches, and other groups could make sure everyone involved was following the same road map.

Joshua stated that as for him and his house, they would follow the Lord. Joshua did not occasionally pray for God's wisdom and then at other times decide to be guided by instinct or public opinion. The direction was always God's way, and everyone in Joshua's household understood that. The subject was not open for debate.

Following God's direction led Joshua and his followers to one victory after another until they possessed the Promised Land. How sad that the previous generation had failed to follow its leader, Moses, in trusting God's guidance. Instead, the people fixed their sights on multiple stars—disobedience, false gods, lack of sacrifice and prayer—resulting in aimless wanderings and eventual death in the desert. The Magi were wiser. They were like David, who asserted of God, "You make known to me the path of life" (Psalm 16:11).

Second, the Wise Men were *goal-oriented*. They wanted to find the Messiah, and they refused to end their journey until they reached him. Nothing could dissuade them. Herod's deceitful words could not fool them. Journey weariness could not discourage them. Nothing could thwart their quest to see the Messiah face to face.

What would the cause of Christianity be like if thousands of modern Christians had the same zeal the Magi had to seek the Savior? Bible reading would be continual. Prayer would be heartfelt and soul-piercing. Christian service would be tireless.

It can be that way. Isaiah 40:31 promises that those who seek and serve God "will run and not grow weary, they will walk and not be faint." To the Magi, the quest to find Jesus was a stimulating, exciting, and enjoyable challenge. It stirred their souls so mightily, they paid no attention to fatigue. What an example this is to us! How much better it is "to serve . . . with all your heart" (Joshua 22:5) than to endure simply for the sake of duty.

A third observation about the Wise Men is that they were *diligent students of the Scriptures*. They had read the teaching of the prophets and, thus, were able to discern the meaning of the great star in the East. We should be no less diligent in our biblical studies. "I have hidden your word in my heart," wrote the psalmist in Psalm 119:11.

A thorough knowledge of the Bible puts a sword of righteousness in our hands. Jesus quoted Old Testament verses to Satan as a way of rebuffing his temptations in the wilderness. Jesus also quoted Scripture to the rich young ruler, to the Jewish elders, and to the lawyers who tried to confront him with tradition rather than laws. Jesus' use of the Scriptures sets a good example for us.

The Magi were futurists; the Scriptures had told them what to look for. With lessons from the Bible, we can also be futurists. There are no surprises to the student of God's Word, for God is the beginning and the end of all things. And he has seen fit to reveal his wisdom to us through his Word. Modern wise men still turn to it.

Finally, the Wise Men were *seeking truth and goodness*. They were not naive about the fact that Israel was an evil and backslidden nation; however, they were confident the Messiah would provide truth and goodness.

Today, we live in a time of wars on numerous continents, civil strife in countless nations, and perversion of endless varieties in all cities. If we do not turn to Christ and see him as an unwavering standard of truth and goodness, we will lose all perspective of what personal dignity is. Jesus was the only person of human flesh "who had no sin" (2 Corinthians 5:21). He was God on Earth. Furthermore, he said, "I am . . . the truth" (John 14:6), and he walked and talked accordingly. He was and is a flawless model of truth and goodness for us to follow.

The Magi accepted everything about the Messiah on faith. The Bible documents this for us. They sought him continuously, as we should also. They remained faithful to their quest until they saw him face to face. We, too, are on a similar journey with an identical quest: we desire to see him one day face to face.

It would be foolish not to trust Christ as our Savior, not to see him as the only righteous standard of religious purity, and not to seek him daily . . . and Wise Men are never foolish.

This is one of the reasons you are reading this book. You want to know how Jesus would handle any incident in life and business. You are seeking him, and that is wise. Now, you must learn how to stay true to your quest.

Gaining Forward Momentum

One of my favorite verses in the King James Version of the Old Testament is Isaiah 62:10: "Go through the gates; prepare ye the way of the people; cast up, cast up the highway; gather out the stones; lift up a standard for the people."

That opening challenge of "Go through the gates" is a call to get started, to do something, to make a mark. We do this by setting proper goals. I have a friend named Bob Rockey who is an avid golfer. He told me an interesting story once. He and three other golfers were on the seventh hole at a lovely course in South Carolina. One of the golfers in Bob's group was an amateur, a teenager still learning the basics of golf. When the foursome came to the green, they told the amateur player to take the flag out of the hole and to set it aside. What they meant was for him to lay it down, which is standard procedure. However, the young man took the flag aside and stuck it in the sand trap to get it out of the way.

JESUS ON SETTING AND REACHING GOALS

Meanwhile, another group of four golfers was just approaching the seventh hole. As they teed up for their opening drives, they sighted the flag that was standing in the sand trap. Each man drove his ball that way . . . and wound up in the sand. When they walked up and discovered what had happened, they were outraged. The amateur golfer apologized profusely, but it was too late. He had already ruined the good scores of the other four golfers.

Too many times people are just like that. They are focused on poorly placed flags in their lives. They set goals that are shallow, simplistic, unworthy, or harmful, and when they reach them and discover they are in a "trap," it's too late to alter the "course" they've laid out for themselves. Their aim was perfect, but their goals were all wrong.

We need to know the proper direction for our lives. If we go up to a ticket master at Grand Central Station and say, "Give me a ticket," she will ask, "Where do you want to go?" If we cannot give an answer better than, "Away from here," she won't be able to put us on the right track. We need to know where we are headed in life.

Do people know where they are going in life? Some years ago I took some of my college writing students to a busy shopping mall in Fort Wayne, Indiana. At random, they stopped one hundred people who were employed at various jobs and asked three simple questions. First, "Would you like to be successful in your career?" and all one hundred people responded, "Yes . . . sure . . . of course . . . naturally." Then they asked, "Are you as successful now as you are ever going to be?" All one hundred responded with something to the effect of, "Gosh, I hope not . . . please, it's got to get better than this . . . no way . . . surely this isn't all life has to offer me." And, finally, the students asked the strangers, "Okay, if it isn't as good now as you want it to be, just when exactly is life going to get better for you?" Of the one hundred people surveyed, only three knew exactly when their lives were going to improve. The others were just hoping against hope that somehow, some way, at some time, life would get better. But just hoping won't make it happen.

Marketing Your Weaknesses

Too many times, people fail to set challenging goals, because they think they are incapable of rising to heights of great success. They believe themselves to be so full of weaknesses, they must be second-rate, low-class also-rans. Ironically, in the world of commercial advertising, many companies have risen to levels of incredible success by trumpeting their so-called "weaknesses."

Years ago, when Coca-Cola, Pepsi-Cola, Diet-Rite Cola, and Royal Crown Cola were dominating the soft-drink market, the company who makes 7-Up started to label its soft drink "The Uncola." It emphasized its "crystal clear, delicious, lemon-lime, sparkling taste." This was so radical an approach to selling soft drinks, it caught on quickly, and sales of 7-Up skyrocketed. Little ol' 7-Up didn't try to imitate the big cola producers. Instead, it proclaimed its uniqueness.

Similarly, Avis Rent A Car ran an ad campaign years ago in which it confessed, "We're only no. 2; we try harder." Avis freely admitted it didn't have as many customers or as many outlets as Hertz, so, as a result, the Avis people worked extra hard to win customers. This approach appealed to people who liked to cheer on underdogs. Soon, Avis was doing more

JESUS ON SETTING AND REACHING GOALS

business than it could handle. And the joke of it was, when the company launched that campaign, it actually wasn't the second most successful rental car company in America. Alamo, National, Budget, and others were ahead of it. However, Avis rose to number two in status thanks to its clever ad campaign. Another good example was the launching of US Airways. It had the guts to call itself, "The No-Frills Airline." In its ads it said passengers wouldn't get in-flight movies or hot meals or beverages or magazines or music or pillows or blankets. Nope, all that passengers would get would be the rock-bottom lowest prices on flights between one city and another. And, crazy as that may seem, lots of people loved that concept. College kids wanting to get to Florida during spring break needed low fares. Senior citizens on limited incomes needed low fares. Members of the military wanting to get home on leave needed low fares. These people weren't interested in movies or magazines—they were interested in fast transportation with the least cost. The ad campaign was a huge success.

Jesus used this same approach many times during his ministry. He taught his disciples not to lament over what they perceived as shortcomings and inabilities, but, instead, to put all their energy into what they *did* have and what they *could* do. When they came to him saying the five thousand people who had come to hear Jesus preach were hungry, Jesus asked them what they had. They replied they had virtually nothing, merely five loaves and two fish. Jesus, however, told them their math was wrong. What they actually had were five loaves, two fish, and the power of the Lord. When they "recalculated," they discovered they actually had too much food and had to spend time picking up all the leftovers after everyone was too full to eat any more.

How Hard Do You Try?

I see people who are perfectly healthy and residing in a prosperous country such as America, yet they "exist" on food stamps and welfare. They complain that life is just too hard. Really? I think of Helen Keller, who went blind and deaf before the age of two. At age twenty-one she wrote her life story, and it became an international best-selling book. At twenty-four she graduated *cum laude* from Radcliffe College with honors in English, German, and French literature. She lived to be eighty-eight and never asked for handouts.

It is consistency of effort that results in achievement. When my son Nathan was a little fellow, I was a leader in his Boys Stockade group at our church. One year I wanted to give a visual lesson to the boys about consistency. On the first night we got together, I showed them a wooden plank that was an inch thick and eighteen inches long. I took out a tiny penknife and I cut a scratch across the plank. The next week, I took the little penknife and I traced the previous week's scratch in a cutting motion. I did this every week, and eight months later, as we were getting ready to stop meeting for the summer, I took out the penknife, ran it along the groove I had been cutting each week, and the 1-inch board split and fell into two pieces. The boys were amazed at what that little blade could do just by "staying at it."

When even "average" people become motivated, they astound themselves at what they can achieve. In the eighteenth century, Robert Owen bought a cotton mill. From a platform on high he observed his employees as they worked at their looms and other machines for one week. At the end of that week, Owen walked through the factory and tied red, green, and yellow ribbons on each loom. Red meant "above average." Green meant "average." Yellow meant "below average." He did not threaten to fire anyone, and he did not offer to give bonuses or raises to anyone. Nevertheless, within two months, all the machines and looms in the factory had red ribbons on them, and morale was never higher. Sometimes, people just need to be recognized, appreciated, and stimulated in order to excel.

Setting the Example

The next part of Isaiah 62:10 says, "Prepare ye the way of the people." By this, I feel Isaiah is admonishing us to set a good example for others to follow. I worked as the public information officer for four years at a small, private Christian college. It was decided the college needed a new gymnasium. A funding campaign was launched to raise three million dollars. Our college president and his wife pledged $10,000 to that campaign. This absolutely stunned me, for I knew the modest salary the president was paid each year. I approached him after a meeting one day and said, "Sir, how can you afford to make such a large pledge to this campaign?" He looked me straight in the face and said, "If I'm going to ask others to give sacrificially, how can I not make such a pledge?"

To me, that was a first-rate effort. It's important to realize how vital first-rate efforts are. In history, we study the names and achievements of people who achieved great "firsts." We know that Charles Lindbergh was the first person to fly solo across the Atlantic, but we don't know (or care) who was second. We know that Edmund Hillary was the first person to conquer Mount Everest, but we don't know or care who was second. We know that George Washington was the first commanding general of the Continental Army, but we don't know or care who was second. And that leads me to ask you these questions: How first-rate is your walk? Who is the first person your friends think of when they need sound advice, spiritual insights, and solid wisdom? Is it you? Have you earned that position of honor? If not, what is lacking in your life that makes you the forgotten runner-up?

Cutting Your Own Trail

The third part of Isaiah 62:10 says, "Cast up, cast up the highway." To me, that means to step forward and blaze a path, even if it means cutting through the maze of a jungle (which I did plenty of during my year as a sergeant in Vietnam) or mushing through a snow-laden trail or traversing a mountain.

I'm sure you've heard many clichés about winning life's journey, e.g., "Inch by inch, anything's a cinch" . . . "The longest journey begins with one step." Clichés usually endure because there is some element of truth to them. To those who feel defeated and weighed down, Jesus promises he will be there to help carry the load. In Matthew 11:28–30, Jesus says, "Come to me, all you who are weary and burdened, and I will give you rest. Take my yoke upon you and learn from me, for I am gentle and humble in heart, and you will find rest for your souls. For my yoke is easy and my burden is light." It's nice to know that as we build up the highway of our life's journey, we have a guide who can show us the straight and narrow way.

Appreciating Struggles

The fourth part of Isaiah 62:10 commands us to "Gather out the stones." In the old days when main thoroughfares were traveled

JESUS ON SETTING AND REACHING GOALS

by a burro or a donkey, the village people tried to keep the paths raked free of rocks so the animals would not stumble, trip, or misstep, possibly being injured. Isaiah is saying we should do the same. If there are stumbling blocks in our way—sins that could or do taint our testimony or hamper our relationship with God—they need to be gathered up and pitched aside.

It's a funny thing about stones. You can learn a lot from them regarding seemingly insurmountable challenges in life. If you hold a small pebble close to your eye, it will fill your entire view, blocking out the entire world. However, if you hold it at arm's length and get some perspective on its weight and size, you'll see that it isn't nearly as "monumental" as you had thought. And, if you toss it to the ground and let it lie at your feet, where it belongs, it will hardly qualify as a bump in the road.

Life's struggles are often similar to that pebble. I've seen college students so obsessed with passing an important exam, they will go without sleep or food or even bathing, just so they can keep pounding the books. I will sometimes intervene and say, "Hey, if you pass the test but have a nervous breakdown, you won't have accomplished anything. It's just one test. Your health, on the other hand, is your entire life. Eat some breakfast, take a shower, grab a short nap, and then get up and review your notes and go pass the test." Once they put that pebble at a proper distance, they do much better.

This is not to say the stones of life are to be ignored. On the contrary, sometimes those rough patches in the road can serve to strengthen us. A bit of struggling is part of God's plan to prepare us to face the world head-on. I recall an incident that bore this out when I was serving as chairman of the school board of Immanuel Christian Elementary School. Our kindergarten class had a terrarium in which the teacher had placed some cocoons and chrysalises she had gathered from a nearby forest. She told the children the caterpillars had woven themselves inside and were turning into beautiful butterflies. Each day the children watched closely. After a time, the cocoons started to wiggle, and the teacher told the children the butterflies were getting ready to break out. During recess, one of the students came back into the class. He reached inside the terrarium and broke open a cocoon. To his horror, an underdeveloped, wet, sticky, still-folded butterfly came out and died. The teacher came into the room and saw what had happened. The little boy held up the dead butterfly and started crying. "I only wanted to help it," he said. "I only wanted to help it." He didn't realize that the struggle was part of God's plan of building strength for what lay ahead.

Sometimes our "breakout" moments are what define us. Picking up a college degree is a breakout moment that will define the rest of a person's life, but it requires four years of struggle beforehand. Being handed a pin with an eagle, globe, and anchor on it is a breakout moment announcing that a person is now a US Marine, but it requires three extremely rigorous months of struggle before it is earned. Retiring with a 401(k) worth half a million dollars is a breakout moment, but it requires decades of struggles at working, saving, and investing in order to make it happen.

Some people don't realize that the struggles are ongoing. A story is told of a seventeen-year-old girl who was seated at a dinner table next to Albert Einstein. She turned to him and asked, "And what do you do?" Einstein responded humbly, "I'm engaged in the study of physics." The girl nodded nonchalantly and said, "Oh, really? I already studied that last semester."

Rather than committing to casting the stones continually

out of the way, many people try to take shortcuts. They don't want to expend the effort needed to make the road smoother in "the long run"—but they eventually discover they've placed themselves on a rocky path. The simple fact is, you have to put something in before you can get something out. My daughter Jeanette discovered this when she was only five. She was given a little gumball machine by her grandmother for her birthday. Jeanette figured out a way to tilt the machine a certain way so it would give out a gumball without first making her insert a penny. Two weeks later, when the gumballs were all gone, Jeanette cried because there was no money in the machine to use to buy a new supply of gumballs. Put nothing in, you get nothing out. (I hired her to pick up all the fallen crabapples in our yard, a job she truly hated. After two hours of that, she was willing to insert a penny each time she wanted a treat.)

Become a Beacon

Isaiah's fifth and final admonition is, "Lift up a standard for the people." By this, I believe he is telling us to serve as a constant rallying point for those around us. Jesus called himself a rallying point. "And I, when I am lifted up from the earth, will draw all people to myself," he said in John 12:32.

I can recall how my two kids, when they were little, would keep their eyes peeled when we were traveling. Once they spotted "the golden arches," they both would start saying, "Mom, Dad, there's McDonald's! Let's go there for lunch." Those golden arches, visible from a distance, helped them zoom in on their destination.

History is filled with incidents of raised standards. Moses lifted the bronze snake in the wilderness. Francis Scott Key wrote about the star-spangled banner that was still flying after a long night of bombardment. The Marines lifted the flag over Mount Suribachi during the battle for Iwo Jima to signal their victory. The American flag was hoisted high above the ruins of the World Trade Center after 9/11 to signal a conquering spirit. Truly, people need rallying points, lifted standards, things to believe in, to focus upon. Proverbs 29:18 says, "Where there is no vision, the people perish" (KJV).

Being able to lift a standard is part of what makes us noble in our work efforts. I recall Senator Robert Kennedy paraphrasing George Bernard Shaw: "There are those who look at things the way they are, and ask why . . . I dream of things that never were, and ask why not." The senator was lifting a standard for us to rally around—something noble, something worthwhile, something positive.

I wonder if we spend enough time looking for righteous standards being lifted before us by God. When Moses sent twelve spies into the Promised Land, ten came back with reports of walled cities and giants. Only two men, Joshua and Caleb, actually saw what the Lord had placed before them—"a land flowing with milk and honey."

We need to have open eyes for standards before us, and we need to be eager to lift God-honoring standards of our own.

"You deliver your water at noon?" asked Jesus.

The woman turned, surprised to find anyone in the building's basement at lunchtime. Normally by now everyone was gathered in the dining commons on the third floor.

"Yes, usually," she responded. "It's easiest if I just slip in when no one is here. I can refill the vending machines and be gone without bothering anyone." She gave him a smile.

"You mean you can avoid being seen," he said flatly.

The woman squinted, more closely examining the face of the stranger. "It's you," she said softly.

"May I have a bottle of water?" he asked.

Without hesitating, she reached for a plastic bottle, then paused. "You own this place. Surely you have a full refrigerator in your office. You don't need water from a vending machine stocker like me."

"All right, then, would you like to come to my office and let me give water to you?"

She knew men. She knew their come-on lines, their pick-up tactics. But this man showed no such ploys. He was sincere. Genuine. It disarmed her. Why, she wondered, would a corporate CEO give the time of day to a vending machine attendant?

"Thanks," she said, "but I'd better get going."

For some reason she felt compelled to fasten one more button on her shirt's open neck. Overt seduction seemed tacky and self-demeaning in the presence of this man.

"There's a reason why you don't want to go to the upper levels of this building, isn't there?"

She lowered her eyes slightly. "My route's almost complete. I need to get back home. My husband will be expecting me." She pushed empty boxes into the recycling bin and grabbed her hand truck.

"You wear no wedding band."

That stopped her.

"Well, yeah," she said slowly. "I guess, legally, Hector's more my live-in. We got plans, though. But for now, no, I don't really have a husband."

"And whom are you taking Hector from?"

She flinched at this. "I beg your pardon?"

"You probably should," he agreed. "But we'll get to that later."

"Whaddya mean about taking Hector?"

Jesus gave a slight shrug. "Women despise you. They resent you. Maria in our shipping department was engaged until you wooed her fiancé away. Tina, one of our warehouse managers, still remembers how she lost her high school sweetheart to you. And Lupe, in our . . ."

"Who told you all this?"

"Why? Do you wish to deny it?"

Slowly, she released her grip on the hand truck.

"You . . . you plan to call my boss? I need this job. I've got kids . . . two girls."

"Do you love them?"

She wrinkled her forehead. "My kids? Of course I do."

"Really?" Jesus paused. "Then why are you subjecting them to the same miserable life you were born into and have adopted as your lifestyle?"

Her eyes widened. "What do you know about that?"

"I know about how you grew up wondering who your real father was. I know about how your mother brought her boyfriends home and how they mistreated you. I know about how you scratched one in the face one night, and he retaliated with a knife, leaving scars on your back and arms, and that's why you wear long-sleeved shirts even in summer."

Instinctively, she shrank into her clothing, as though suddenly exposed. "What's this all about?"

Jesus smiled kindly. "You."

"Me?"

"And your children." *He pulled a chair away from a metal table and sat, keeping some distance between himself and the woman.* "Sit for a minute, Juanita."

This caught her attention.

"How do you know my name? I've never met you. I don't know you."

"No . . . no, you don't. But I'm hoping we can change that. Anyway, as for your name, in case you've forgotten, it's sewn on your company jacket."

She looked down and saw JUANITA in bold yellow letters. She shook her head. "Oh. That. For a minute, I thought you were some kind of a mind reader."

"I'm better at hearts. And yours is hurting."

She was silent a moment. She eased into the chair he had pointed at. "I do okay."

"No, you don't," *he said nonjudgmentally.* "You feel like used goods. It's not just your body that's scarred, it's your soul. You feel ugly, marred, battered. You long for genuine love, but you don't feel worthy of it. So, instead, you try to seduce men, lure them away from other women, using any means in your power. It convinces you that you are as good as they are, as feminine and as attractive and as pure.

"But it's all a vicious cycle. After you've cheapened yourself to win a man's attention, he has less respect for you than you even have for yourself. He eventually walks out on you, leaving you feeling worse than ever, so you go out seeking someone else.

It's been like this for years. Broken relationships, children born out of wedlock, physical and emotional abuse. It really needs to stop. That's no way to live."

Nothing was said for a full minute. Soon, tears on Juanita's face betrayed her emotion. She dabbed impatiently at them with her sleeve.

"I should be afraid," she said quietly. "I don't know how you know all this. You know everything about me." Slowly, she looked up. "But I'm not afraid. You don't scare me. I feel relieved . . . like someone has finally . . . finally. . . ."

"Read your heart?"

She nodded.

He gave her time. Neither felt rushed. Minutes passed. The room remained silent and empty, save for the two of them.

"You are a wise man. You know things. I'm a troubled woman. I wonder, Is there hope for me, for my children? Is there another way of life, and how do you get there? I want so much for my girls to have a better life than I had. I don't want them to . . . to go the way I've gone."

"You're a water delivery woman who is thirsty for a new way of life. I have a different kind of water for you. It cleanses. It restores. It refreshes and renews. But it's not for you alone. Get out your cell phone. Call Hector. Tell him to come here, now, and to bring your two little girls with him. Life is about to change for all of you, if you truly seek a change."

Juanita eagerly found her phone and started to dial. Midway, she stopped. She stood and walked toward Jesus. "After we have talked—all of us—I need to do something. But, I'll need your strength."

Jesus gently touched one of her shoulders.

JESUS ON SETTING AND REACHING GOALS

"Yes," he assured her. "I'll go upstairs with you to see Maria and Tina and Lupe. I will help you make things right with them." Juanita was not amazed at his words. She only smiled. She finished dialing the number.

Section 7

What Jesus Taught about Diversified Portfolios

The reason Jesus spoke so much about money matters is because, quite frankly, money matters. More than two thousand verses in the New Testament refer to money or material possessions. That's four times as many verses as those that relate to heaven or hell. Of Christ's thirty-eight parables, sixteen relate to various financial matters.

Everyone needs money, and it's time some Christian said it out loud. I don't mind being first: *Christians need money, just like everyone else!* There is nothing holy about poverty, and there is nothing evil about wealth.

Having written two books and numerous articles on Christian approaches to financial management, I have often encouraged people to develop a diversified financial portfolio. I've recommended that people create a good balance among real estate, stocks, bonds, bank accounts, and other investment vehicles.

Acquiring adequate funds to care properly for yourself and your family is God-honoring and proper. But, at best, these accumulations will only be "short-term" investments. Compared with eternity, a human lifetime disappears like a mist (James 4:14). Therefore, of even greater importance than having a diversified financial portfolio is the need to develop a diversified *spiritual* portfolio.

As Christians we are directed to establish our personal treasures "in heaven" (Matthew 19:21); however, the interest and other earnings from these treasures (the "fruits" of our special investments) are to be disbursed here on Earth (John 15:16).

Creating Spiritual Portfolios

I've known many people who had very little in the way of material wealth, yet were possessors of abundantly rich spiritual portfolios. They developed these portfolios by diversifying their investments and allowing the benefits to compound continuously.

Here's how you can do the same thing. First, make a list of what assets you have to invest for the cause of Christ. Among other things, you have time, money, prayer, mentoring, and witnessing. Additionally, you may have other spiritual gifts, such as singing, writing, preaching, or teaching.

Next, determine whether you are giving time to several of these abilities of yours or whether you are simply emphasizing one. If you donate money to the church, that is a blessing; but without prayer support, the job is only half done. Similarly, if you witness to an unbeliever and win him or her to the Lord, but then do not continue to mentor, encourage, and nurture that person, the chance for spiritual growth will be diminished greatly.

WHAT JESUS TAUGHT ABOUT DIVERSIFIED PORTFOLIOS

The Big Payoff

In the world of finance, when a dollar is invested at good rates over a period of years, profits will be great. But it takes all three elements to generate these profits (money, time, good rates).

Having *money* to invest and *time* to wait is of no value unless *rates* are strong and steady. To guarantee that such rates will always be high, investors diversify their portfolios. Thus, when real-estate earnings are low, investors put their money into stocks; and, if bond prices fall, investors switch their money into gold coins or art objects. No matter what the situation is, wise portfolio managers always strive to get a good return on their investments.

The returns on spiritual investments work the same way. When one redeemed soul invests his or her abilities in a variety of ways throughout the course of a lifetime, the overall gains are astounding. A diversified spiritual portfolio always prospers. If a person is temporarily not in a position to support the church monetarily, that person can still make investments of prayer time or personal witnessing. If a person's voice becomes too frail to sing, that doesn't prevent his or her hand from writing notes of welcome to church visitors. Investment opportunities are always available.

Financial investors know that a dollar earned as interest has the ability to earn a dollar of its own, and so on. Likewise, one believer who converts a lost soul to Christ can expect that convert to reach a convert of his or her own, and so on. Over time, from one person's conversion until the end of that person's life, this "compounding effect" can result in amazing growth.

Whether or not you have the financial savvy to become a wealthy tycoon, you can amass great riches in heaven. For the latter, all you need is to recognize the assets you have for investing in the cause of Christ. The more you utilize, the greater the return on your overall investments.

So, *recognize* your diversified abilities, *capitalize* on your opportunities, and *profit* from your investments. One day, it will make you one of the "redeemed" in Christ . . . in more ways than one.

It was almost midnight when Jesus came out the side exit of his corporate building. He spoke briefly to the night watchman, then stepped out onto the sidewalk. Half a block away under the streetlights, three large black limousines with tinted windows were parked in single file. The back door of the first vehicle opened suddenly, and two burly men in dark windbreakers stepped out. They surveyed the area, then nodded.

Men emerged from the third car, came to the middle car, and opened the back door. A tall, gaunt man, dressed in a hand-tailored pinstripe suit emerged. He began to walk directly toward Jesus, his entourage of bodyguards surrounding him.

"Sir," the man called out, "may I have a word with you?"

Jesus smiled as the group approached. "Am I so threatening, you need an army around you? Send these men away."

The stranger hesitated, then slowly waved his men back to the limos. "May I invite you into my car?" he suggested. "I have refreshments."

"Thank you, no," said Jesus. "Let's walk." He turned and ambled up the street. The man followed.

"You don't seem taken aback that someone would come to see you at midnight."

WHAT JESUS TAUGHT ABOUT DIVERSIFIED PORTFOLIOS

"People come to me at all hours of the day and night," said Jesus. "It would surprise you. But for right now, let's focus on you, Mr. Demos."

The man nodded. "Yes, I assumed you'd recognize me. My face has been on the cover of every major business magazine at least twice this year already. That's why I came to see you at night. It's the only way I can be guaranteed some privacy."

Jesus stopped and turned to face the man. "No, you came to see me at night because you didn't want to be seen talking with me. You are Nicolas Demos, executive extraordinaire, and you take advice from no one, least of all a 32-year-old furniture maker."

Demos gave a twisted smile. "I'd heard you were a man who was not to be underestimated. I apologize. You're right. I do worry about my image, my reputation. I mean no disrespect to you, however. If it's all right with you, I'd like to ask you some questions."

"I baffle you, don't I, Nick?" Jesus started to walk again. The limos, their engines purring, began to follow at a safe distance.

"You do, sir. You do, indeed."

"You've studied me, you've analyzed my company, yet you can't put the pieces together. You've done hostile takeovers. You've led stock revolts. You've run little companies out of business, and you've beaten big companies to market with key products. In each case, you studied your adversary, found his weaknesses, exploited them, and emerged victorious."

"You paint me as rather cold-hearted and calculating."

"You're the one who referred to the business articles written about you. Read them. You're wealthy, but you're loathed. In fact, you despise yourself to some degree. That's why you're here tonight."

Demos lifted one hand dramatically. "I wouldn't say I despise myself."

"I said it for you," said Jesus. He stopped walking and moved in close to the other man. *"It's late. Let me save us some time. You don't want to take over my company. You don't need another business. What you do want is to discover why my company runs so smoothly, so efficiently, so lovingly."*

"Lovingly?" injected Demos. "Odd choice of a word."

"Odd for business textbooks, maybe. Odd for corporate year-end reports. Odd for business seminars. But not odd for what we do at my company. Your businesses are sterile. They're inflexible. They're static. The same goes for you. The reason you take over other businesses is because you have no natural creativity, no imagination, no sense of innovation."

"Actually, I've been praised for my portfolio diversification," said Nick. "I'm engaged in a wide variety of corporate lines."

Jesus shook his head. "Don't delude yourself. You usurp other people's achievements and discoveries. But when you look in the mirror at the end of each day, you know you're dry. You're flat. You're a man who desperately wants to be admired as a craftsman, a designer, an artisan, but, for a fact, you're nothing but a leech."

The two men stared at each other without blinking for what seemed like endless minutes.

Finally, Demos averted his gaze, moved to a sidewalk bench and slumped down. "How . . . how do you know these things?"

"How do you not *know them?" Jesus seated himself next to Nick.*

Nothing was said. Nick stared ahead, as if in a trance, as though trying to see beyond the veil of night.

"I used to draw," he said at last. "Back in high school. I

took art classes, and I even won a best of show when I was only 14. My teachers praised me, said I had a good eye for depth and color and balance. My mother hung my drawings and paintings all over our home. She bragged about me to all her friends."

"But your father didn't," Jesus pointed out softly.

"No," agreed Nick, equally softly. "Not my father. I was his only son, and he was determined I was going to take over the family enterprises one day. Art could be a rich man's hobby at some later date, but first came accounting, law, economics, and marketing. And so it was. I suppressed my creative impulses and focused on logic, pragmatism, and profitability."

"And what shall it profit a man if he gains the whole world and loses his soul?"

"What, indeed?" agreed Nick.

"You need to be reborn."

"Say again?"

"Go back to your mother. Ask her for all your drawings and paintings from when you were in high school. Become a kid again. Start fresh. Look at the artwork and then look into your heart, your soul. Grab a sketch pad and start drawing. Pick up where you left off."

"I'm old. How can I become a teenager again?"

"You're worse than old," said Jesus. "You're dead. But if you listen to me and do as I say, you can be born again. Will you trust me?"

Nick smiled sardonically. "My father would roll over in his grave if he heard this conversation."

"No," said Jesus, "I'm still the only one who can do that. But, here we digress. I ask you again, will you trust me? Will you start your life over? Be born again?"

Nick shrugged. "The life I'm living is doing nothing for me. Who knows? Maybe I still have a few landscapes and portraits in me. Whatever happens, at least I'll be having some fun again."

"I'll hire you," said Jesus.

Nick stood still, not comprehending. "You'll what?"

"I'll hire you," repeated Jesus. "I have a large wall in our company reception area. It has never been thoroughly cleaned since I originally bought the building. I want you, personally, to wash it as white as snow. Then I want you to paint a relaxing scene on it. Show me some green pastures, some still waters . . . some paths of righteousness."

"Some what?*"*

Jesus grinned. "Just go with what comes naturally to you. Rediscover your passion. You'll do fine."

"You're serious? You really are going to trust me to paint a mural in your reception area?"

"I am," Jesus assured him, rising and turning to walk away. "With one proviso."

Nick's eyes narrowed. "Which would be . . . ?"

"That from now on," said Jesus, "you come around during the day."

Section 8

JESUS ON ACCEPTING A PERSONAL CALLING

People want to know what life is all about. I know the answer, and I'm going to tell it to you now.

Let me explain how I discovered it. I had been a writer for several years. I'd interviewed successful people in all walks of life—industry, medicine, sports, science, law, entertainment, communications, entrepreneurship, politics. Subconsciously, I began picking up on some commonalities among these leaders—these winners, these champions.

They could work twelve hours a day and not show fatigue. They remained optimistic when others became depressed. What some people viewed as failure, they saw as forward momentum on the learning curve. These people simply did not know how to quit. Mind you, I did not say they did not know how to *fail*— in fact, they failed quite often—but what they did not know how to do was *quit*.

After I examined these astounding people for many years, their secret of success came to me one day as a grand epiphany: *These people never went to work a day in their lives!* What they did was discover the one thing that excited them the most, and then they spent the rest of their lives in all-out pursuit of it.

When I interviewed Loretta Lynn, she told me that nothing made her happier when she was a kid than to belt out hillbilly tunes for her relatives. They would applaud her and cheer her until she forgot she was poor, forgot she lacked formal education, and forgot she was dressed in rags. She knew she was destined to sing . . . and sing she did. And her charisma and verve and energy were so contagious, crowds swarmed to hear her. Some years after she became a famous recording artist, she would do up to 255 concerts per year. To others, such a grueling schedule of road tours would have been torture, but to Loretta, it was just singing—and singing made her deliriously happy. Even after she had millions of dollars, she continued to sing. It was never about the money; it was always about the singing.

In a somewhat similar story, when Jerry B. Jenkins was a kid, someone asked him to write up a story about a local sporting event. He did, and the city newspaper ran it. Jerry saw his name in print, and he knew that writing was his passion. He threw himself into it, spending the ensuing years doing interviews, writing sports stories, teen mysteries, devotions, biographies—loving the creative process, getting ecstatic each time his byline appeared in print, reveling in the response from readers. Decades later, he wrote the Left Behind series, which sold more than sixty-three million novels, and he became the most successful author in the world for several consecutive years. But he never stopped writing, because it was never about the sales totals; it was always about the writing.

Steve Jobs completely revolutionized computer technology, and had a blast doing it. Michael Jackson totally revamped the venue of modern dance, and never got tired of stunning audiences with new moves. Sally Ride grew up wanting to be the equal of Amelia Earhart, and she wound up turning somersaults in a weightless rocket ship as the first woman in space. Dr. Ben Carson imagined a futuristic world in which surgical medicine and scientific hardware could be united to perform miracles, and he became the first physician to separate conjoined twins and have both twins live.

These people discovered their passions, threw themselves into actualizing their dreams, and, in the process, changed the world. And therein lies the basis of what life is all about. Sooner or later, we all become cognizant of what we were put on this earth to do. The brilliant Jewish psychologist Dr. Viktor Frankl, who survived the Nazi death camps and went on to write a series of stirring books that examined all aspects of the human psyche, wrote, "Your meaning will put in an appearance."

I agree with that statement. Many of you now reading this book, no matter your age, have not had your "Ah-ha!" moment yet. My job as your teacher and mentor is to help you discover your destiny. That is why I encourage you to be a searcher. Read books. Listen to audio books. Talk to interesting people. Ask questions. Attend seminars, workshops, and conferences. Study your Bible. If you never allow yourself to be exposed to the full range of career options, there is a good chance you will never have revealed to you the areas in which your gift is meant to flourish. I'm convinced that at any moment your revelation of personal quest may be awakened. What you *do* with that magnificent insight will determine whether you will achieve personal fulfillment or, conversely, if you will lead a life of what Henry David Thoreau labeled "quiet desperation."

And so, true to my promise to you, I now give you the answer to the question, "What is life all about?" *Life* is about understanding the undeniable truth of this five-word statement: *Inspiration without manifestation causes frustration.*

Simply put, once you are *inspired* by what you know—beyond a shadow of a doubt—is your calling in life, you must do everything in your power to *manifest* its fulfillment in your thoughts and deeds, lest you endure a life of *frustrated* incompleteness.

Is Destiny Real?

Can we believe in a sense of destiny? Is there such a thing as being in harmony with the universe?

Can we be utterly confident in thinking that God has a plan for our individual lives?

If so, why is life so hard?

If Joseph was shown early in life that his brothers would bow before him and that it was his future to rise to power and prestige, why did he have to be sold into slavery, then be thrown into prison for seven years before fulfilling his destiny?

If, before Jeremiah was formed in his mother's womb he was destined by God to be the Lord's mouthpiece by age twenty-one, why did he have to endure scoffing, derision, mockery, and ostracism before achieving the undeniable status of prophet?

If John the Baptist was the one anointed to pave the way for the coming ministry of Christ, why was he relegated to being a voice in the wilderness, existing on honey and locusts, later imprisoned, and ultimately beheaded?

Why was Nelson Mandela jailed for decades before fulfilling his destiny of bringing freedom to the oppressed people of South Africa? Why was Martin Luther King, Jr. imprisoned in Birmingham, Alabama, and ultimately assassinated in Memphis,

JESUS ON ACCEPTING A PERSONAL CALLING

Tennessee, while fulfilling his destiny of securing civil rights for people of color in America?

These seem like unsolvable mysteries . . . inexplicable conundrums . . . baffling ironies. But they are not. There is a logic to it all. The Scriptures explain it.

First, life is too short not to go all out to discover, pursue, and fulfill your destiny. James 4:14 tells us, "What is your life? You are a mist that appears for a little while and then vanishes." Seriously, if the earth is 6,000 years old and your life is about eighty years, you've got roughly one percentage point of time to achieve anything. You need to go flat out. People seeking their destiny understand this.

Second, the difficulties and setbacks of life are inconsequential to people with a sense of mission. Job said, "Though he slay me, yet will I hope in him" (Job 13:15). Henry Ford said, "Failure is simply the opportunity to begin again, this time more intelligently." When John Bunyan was put in prison, he used the time to write *Pilgrim's Progress*. When I was in Vietnam for a year, I read one hundred books, watched one hundred movies, learned to speak Vietnamese, earned a brown belt in Taekwondo, and rose to the rank of sergeant while being awarded six combat medals, two unit citations, and five Letters of Commendation.

John Milton wrote in *Paradise Lost*, "You can make a hell of heaven or a heaven of hell depending on your state of mind." So it is with people of destiny. They expect challenges and face them head-on. They adapt, modify, adjust, and improvise. They use every experience as a new point of perspective. (In my line of work we say, "Nothing bad ever happens to a writer. It's all material.") Jesus was not naive about the harsh realities of life. He cautioned, "Be careful, or your hearts will be weighed down with . . . the anxieties of life" (Luke 21:34).

Third, the payoff warrants the sacrifice. People with a sense of mission realize that *delayed gratification* is a discipline required for ultimate success. Paul wrote to Timothy, "Do your best to present yourself to God as one approved, a worker who does not need to be ashamed and who correctly handles the word of truth" (2 Timothy 2:15). Sweat equity is the price of great achievement. The Scriptures say, "A man reaps what he sows" (Galatians 6:7).

Some people sit in front of a stove and say, "Give me heat and I'll give you some wood." Not people of destiny. They throw on wood, coal, gasoline, matches, newspaper, kindling—they are constantly "adding fuel to the fire." They invest, strategize, game plan, exert, push, sustain, drive, advance, build, compound, enhance, and formulate. For them, the mountain's only purpose is to provide the summit's view. The marathon's only function is to allow a bursting through the ribbon. All during the plowing, planting, watering, fertilizing, and weeding, the only thought is of the harvest. The end result—the legacy, the conquest, the achievement—is all that ever matters to people of destiny.

Ending Well

When people of destiny die, they are content. They don't say, "If only I had it to do over. I wish I would have _____." Instead, like Jesus, they have their own version of, "It is finished." Do you think it was mere "coincidence" Thomas Jefferson and John Adams both died on the Fourth of July, 1826, *exactly* one-half century after America had declared independence as a nation? These men died thinking, "We did it! It is accomplished."

JESUS ON ACCEPTING A PERSONAL CALLING

Jesus talked in John 16:33 about people being at peace despite the challenges the world would throw at those who choose to follow a righteous cause: "I have told you these things, so that in me you may have peace. In this world you will have trouble. But take heart! I have overcome the world."

Is any of this to say you won't be amazed—perhaps even temporarily terrified—over your personal call to destiny? Consider it normal.

Wasn't it Moses who said, "Who am I, Lord, that I should go before Pharaoh?"

Didn't Gideon say, "But, Lord, I am from a humble family, in which I, myself, am the humblest"?

Even Isaiah argued, "But, Lord, I am a man of unclean lips."

More often than not, it may be your seeming "weakness" that will make you all the more appealing for God's purpose. When David, a little boy, slew the giant Goliath, it was obvious it was the hand of the Lord at work. The apostle Paul noted, "When I am weak, that's when I am strong," meaning that the more his corporeal strength failed him, the more he was required to call upon the power of God, which only served to make him more forceful and dynamic than ever.

Answering the Call

When Peter and Andrew dropped their nets, left the family fishing business, and followed Jesus, their friends and neighbors must have thought they were crazy. At life's end, however, they were able to calculate that what they *netted* was far greater than clothes that smelled of dead fish and a rotting boat full of leaks. They proved that, if you're going to walk on water, sometimes you first sometimes have to jump ship.

JESUS IN THE 9 TO 5

As you sit where you are this very minute, reading and contemplating my words, consider that my message to you may be the initiation of *your* Esther experience, namely: "Who knows but that you were called for such a time as this?" Maybe you are reading this, right now, to learn that your life is meant to be one of *manifested inspiration* . . . that your dream is not a fantasy but a calling . . . that your exuberant joy is not a time-consuming hobby but a world-changing passion set for volcanic eruption.

What is your burning quest—to be an inventor? To serve as a missionary? To write novels? To perform surgery, teach young children, design great buildings, create new software, form a nonprofit foundation?

Is it a sincere calling? If so, then *attack!* Better to go down in flames than to smolder in "quiet desperation."

Inspiration without manifestation causes frustration.

Inspiration *with* manifestation leads to *destination*.

Don't . . . die . . . frustrated!

Jonathan Markelson was surprised to see the boss seated to one side of the room. It was annual review time for Jon, and he knew he was scheduled to spend half an hour with his regional manager, Paul Stoner. However, having Jesus, the owner of the whole company, also sitting in on the annual review was unexpected, even a bit unsettling.

"Mornin', Jon. Have a seat," greeted Paul. "We're just waiting for one more arrival. I've asked our training director, Barney Gardner, to join us. Had coffee?"

Jon nodded. "I'm fine, Mr. Stoner." He pulled back a chair and sat across the table from Paul. Out of the corner of his eye

JESUS ON ACCEPTING A PERSONAL CALLING

he could see that Jesus was nonchalantly skimming through the contents of some manila folders.

"Two years? Is that about right?"

Jon's head jerked up. "Sorry?"

"Two years," Stoner repeated. "You've been on the road selling our products for about two years now, right?"

"Oh . . . oh, yeah. Two years this month. Yes, sir. I have a three-state region." He then smiled sheepishly. "But . . . you know that."

"Read in the company newsletter you got engaged. Congratulations."

Jon blushed slightly. "Thanks. You know her. It's Lydia. She works in our fabric dyeing department. We're planning on a spring wedding."

"Order plenty of beverages," said Jesus.

Jon was caught off guard by the comment. He shifted slightly in his chair to look toward the boss.

"Beverages, sir?"

"Trust me," said Jesus. "Nothing ruins a wedding faster than running out of beverages."

"Uh . . . yes, sir. Beverages. I'll remember that."

At that moment the meeting room door swung open and banged against the back wall.

Barney Gardner exploded into the room, a giant of a man with a head of dark, stringy curls, and a lumberjack's beard. He was deeply tanned, and his oversized smile revealed dazzling white teeth. His arms were spilling over with folders, computer printout pages, partially folded maps, and date books.

"Sorry if I'm a bit late," Barney announced as he piled his paraphernalia on the table and yanked out a chair. "Came up with an idea for promoting our new deck chairs. Needed to sketch it out and pass it along to the design crew." He looked around. "Things started here yet?"

"Start without you?" said Stoner. "Heaven forbid."

Jesus looked up. "Uh . . . not so far. You fellows go ahead."

Paul Stoner rapped his knuckles twice on the unopened folder before him.

"I spent last night going over your sales records, Jon. I'll tell you flat out, I'm not impressed. Last year when we sat here, you told me you needed more time to work the territory, get to know the buyers, learn more about our products. Well, I gave you that extra year, but I'm not seeing any improvement. What's your problem?"

Jon shifted in his chair. "I work my territories. If you look at my stats, I sell to half the people I call on."

"But, said another way," said Stoner, "you fail to sell to half the people you call on. You were our prototype, our experiment. We've always sold our products by having buyers' reps come to our warehouse and choose models and place orders for their stores. You were the first person we sent out to sell directly to the stores and outlets who weren't doing business with us. It was a great opportunity for you, something cutting-edge, but you dropped the ball. You're a huge disappointment to me."

"I did a pretty decent job of moving our new patio furniture."

Stoner opened the folder. "Yep, you sold the whole line to six department stores, but then you didn't go out on the road again for two weeks." He squinted at his notes. "Make that three weeks."

"It was deer hunting season, and I thought I'd done pretty well," said Jon, "so I figured a week or so at my cabin wouldn't be so bad."

JESUS ON ACCEPTING A PERSONAL CALLING

"That's your problem, Jon. You're unreliable. For a few weeks you work like crazy, but then you disappear for weeks at a time. Accounts need to be serviced. Phone calls need to be returned. Stores need to be visited. You're inconsistent, and I'm afraid that just won't work in an operation like ours."

"Maybe if I worked a little with him . . ." said Barney, with an ingratiating smile.

"You have *worked with him," countered Stoner. "It's done no good. A blind man could see it." He paused, glanced up at the fluorescent light fixture over the table, then cleared his throat. "You'll have to take my word on that one. The point is, if Jon doesn't make his numbers, then I can't make mine." He looked Jonathan straight in the face. "Sorry, Jon, we can't carry you any longer."*

Jon wrinkled his forehead. "What . . . what are you saying?"

"He's saying you're fired," said Jesus flatly. "Turn in your sample cases and clean out your desk by noon, please."

The blood drained from Jon's face. "Fired? I'm . . . I'm fired? Wait . . . no . . . I can't be fired. I'm getting married. We need the money. We've got plans, big plans. I can't tell my fiancée I've lost my job."

"Maybe you'll be fortunate enough to find a new job before she finds out you've lost this one," said Paul Stoner. "I'll need the keys to your company car, too."

Jon backed his chair away and turned his eyes upon Jesus. "I just can't see what I've done that's so bad. You're actually firing me?"

Jesus stood and walked across the room toward Jonathan. He looked down at the young man still seated in the chair. "Here's my problem with you, son. If you were a total loser, never came to work and never made a sale, I could understand that. It would be obvious you were the wrong person for the job. Conversely, if you were here every day, working the phone lines, going out and talking to clients, and closing deals, I could understand that, too. You'd be the top producer in our company. But you're neither cold nor hot. You're neutral. You're an also-ran. You're . . . well, you're a lukewarm body. And lukewarm is something we can't abide around here. Especially me."

Jesus walked out of the room.

Jonathan looked first to Paul Stoner and then to Barney Gardner.

"That's it? I'm done? I put two years of my life into this company and in five minutes you show me the door?"

Paul Stoner squinted. "That's the problem, Jon. You didn't put two years into the job. You gave us a half-baked effort. To be gut honest with you, I wanted to let you go last year, but Barney, here, saw some potential in you. He convinced me to give you another shot. I should have gone with my first decision. Hand me the keys to the company car."

Barney lifted his beefy arms. "Can we slow down a moment here, Paul? Let's look again at Jon's file, see where he has improved, find places where we can help him overcome some shortcomings."

"To coin a phrase," replied Paul, "it is finished."

"There's always room for talk," insisted Barney.

"The boss just said he is lukewarm, and we can't abide that around here. Far be it from me to countermand one of his decisions. If you've got a case to present, you're going to have to go directly to him."

Barney rubbed his forehead and pondered the situation. He looked into the panic-stricken eyes of the young man across the table from him.

JESUS ON ACCEPTING A PERSONAL CALLING

"Can you help me here, Mr. Gardner? I really need this job. I actually thought I was coming in today to get a raise or a promotion. Obviously, I've messed up. But I can change. I promise you I can change. This time I mean it."

"You're going to have to clear out, I'm afraid," said Paul. "I've got more people I have to see today."

Barney stood slowly. He looked at Paul Stoner. "Go on without me for a while. I'm going to see if I can have a word with the boss about poor Jon here."

Paul bristled. "I agree with the boss. The matter has been decided."

"Perhaps. But I still want to see if I can make a case for Jon here."

"Then don't bother coming back," said Paul.

"How's that?"

"I can see we're not of like minds any longer, so I'll handle the year-end reviews and you stick to training. From now on, we'll go our separate ways."

Barney looked genuinely sad. "That grieves me. You're a very hard man at times, Paul. You often forget that you made a lot of mistakes in your youth. There should be more room for empathy in your heart."

"I'll be the first to admit I've been the chief of mistake-makers," said Paul. "But that doesn't give me leeway to allow others to thwart the work we're doing here. Sorry, but my decision stands. Jon is fired . . . unless I hear differently from the boss."

Methodically, Barney picked up his stacks of materials. He gestured for Jonathan to leave the room. Jonathan placed a set of car keys on the table and then followed Barney out into the hallway.

"Go to the employee lounge and wait for me there. I'm going to try to talk to the boss for a few minutes on your behalf. I can't promise you anything, but I'll at least make a case for you. But trust me on one thing. Should you be fortunate enough to get your job back, you'd better produce, mister. If not, then I, personally, will give you the axe."

Without waiting for a response, Barney turned and headed down the hall. He ducked into his small office and dropped all his papers on his desk. He turned to leave and was shocked to find Jesus standing in his doorway, as though he had somehow just materialized out of thin air.

"Coming to see me, were you, Barney?"

Barney shook his head slowly and offered a wry grin. "I've given up trying to figure out how you're always one step ahead of me." He pointed to a chair, then rushed over to remove the stacks of books, catalogs, and file folders piled on it. "If you have a minute?"

Jesus accepted the chair while Barney dropped the clutter onto a bare spot on the floor. Barney moved behind his desk and also sat. "I have a confession to make," Barney began.

"Jonathan Markelson is your mother's sister's late-in-life child," Jesus interrupted. "He's seventeen years younger than you, but he's still your cousin."

Barney's eyes widened. He slowly eased back into his leather chair. "So! You've known all along." He unconsciously stroked his thick beard. "I should have guessed I couldn't hide something like that from you. Ha—it's like you've known everyone since the womb."

"Yeah," said Jesus. "Almost like that, isn't it?"

"Jon's father died of cancer some years ago. I've been trying to serve as kind of a surrogate dad to him. He's a good

JESUS ON ACCEPTING A PERSONAL CALLING

kid, really, but still green. Not to second-guess you, Boss, but I thought you and Paul were a bit harsh on the boy earlier today."

"A workman is worthy of his hire only if he earns it."

"Yes, yes, I totally agree. But in this case, I feel some of the blame needs to be put on my shoulders. If I had just coached the boy a little more . . . if I had monitored his behavior a bit more . . ."

"I've heard Paul Stoner admonish our younger employees," countered Jesus. "He tells them that when he was a kid, he did childish things. However, now that he's a man, he has put childish things aside. There's a time to play and a time to work."

Barney raised his hands in surrender. "I have no counterpoint to anything you're saying. Instead, I am going to ask for temporary leniency. Jon is bearing no fruit, but I know his heritage. His roots are solid. Let me do a little spade work with him. There are some fertile sales territories I can work him into. I'll work beside him. I'll be his rainmaker until he starts to blossom on his own."

"And what if, even then, he doesn't perform?"

"I've already told him, I'll cut him off at the knees myself. One year, that's all I'm asking. One more year, and if he doesn't produce, I'll personally drop him."

Jesus stood. "You're a good man, Barney. All right, I'll grant the year. You realize, however, this is going to create some bad blood between you and Paul."

"It already has," said Barney. "But I've got a solution to that."

"Tell me."

"Paul is a hard man, but totally fair. I figure that if I can help Jon reestablish himself as a dedicated, hard worker, Paul will one day accept him back on the team. It's going to require a lot of effort, but that's my goal."

"Hmmm . . . sure," said Jesus, with a satisfied look on his face. "I can see that happening. Not a bad plan. Not a bad plan at all."

Section 9

TIME MANAGEMENT CONCEPTS SHARED BY JESUS

Scripture tells us there is a time for every purpose under heaven (Ecclesiastes 3:1). This would indicate that life flows in a series of sequences: winter, spring, summer, fall; planting, watering, growing, harvesting; dawn, day, sunset, night.

Jesus' time on Earth was limited, so the call to "redeem the time" was something he shared often. However, Jesus was not constrained by time. He knew when to withdraw alone to pray and meditate. He knew how to complete a task at hand, even if it meant not responding to other people's demands on his time (including not rushing to the aid of his friend Lazarus, who was dying). He knew how to prioritize time, as when he told Martha that Mary's time was better spent listening to his teachings than working in a kitchen fixing a meal. He knew how to adjust time to accommodate others, as when he said his time "had not yet come," but allowed his mother to convince him to perform the miracle of turning water into wine at a friend's wedding. Most important of all, he knew how to achieve lifetime goals so he could say, "It is finished" with a sense of having accomplished all his Father had sent him to do.

Knowing this, it seems appropriate we, too, should place a value on the time of our lives. I've frequently led workshops on the subject of time management at many schools, companies, and corporations. How odd it strikes me when someone comes up to me and says, "I'm going to spend some time studying time management . . . just as soon as I can find the time to get around to it." Whether you recognize it or not, you are having "the time of your life" this very moment. The average person is allotted "threescore years and ten" (Psalm 90:10), which isn't very long. It behooves us to make the most of it.

I could devote an entire book to the study of time management (I know—I've done it twice). But let me condense a broad range of knowledge into a succinct alphabet of tips that will help you become better organized and more productive.

(A) **Audio Learning**—Use commuting time and exercise time to listen to audio books that can teach you a new language, show you how to improve customer service, motivate you to work harder, or explain innovative business techniques. Don't simply settle for being entertained by music, games, or videos.

(B) **Building Slack Time**—Plan some extra time into your daily schedule (one open appointment, a shorter lunch hour) so unforeseen interruptions do not cause a panic.

(C) **Capturing Thoughts and Ideas**—Carry two books with you at all times: one to read when you are caught with time on your hands and one with blank pages so you can write down any good ideas you suddenly develop. Instead of paper books, you can also use your

TIME MANAGEMENT CONCEPTS SHARED BY JESUS

favorite electronic devices to help you perform these time-saving functions.

(D) **Deciding Your Actions**—Learn to make a decision: to lead, follow, or get out of the way.

(E) **Efficiently Arranging Space**—If you work in an office or a work cubicle, arrange all your furniture and equipment so you can reach items with a minimum of effort. Without having to stand, you should be able to reach your wastebasket, in/out trays, computer, scanner, bulletin board, and phone.

(F) **Five-Minute Pausing**—Instead of long coffee breaks, take five-minute work pauses. This will refresh you but not cause you to lose your work inertia or project momentum.

(G) **Game-Planning**—Game-plan your 24-hour time periods by filling out a "To Do" list each night before bed. Stick to your game plan each day. As you complete each job, cross it off as a psychological reward.

(H) **Healthy Living**—Stay healthy. Take vitamins, get regular exercise, eat nutritious foods, control your weight, and get regular dental and medical checkups. Time spent in sickbeds or in hospital wards is wasted time.

(I) **Involving Inanimate Assistance**—If you can afford them, use machines and electronics that will save you time.

(J) **Just Saying "No"**—Learn to say "no" without feeling guilty. If you are asked to perform a job you know you don't have time to do to the best of your ability, say "no." You do more damage by doing something halfway than by refusing to get involved in the first place.

(K) **Keeping Goals**—Set goals and strive to reach them by specific dates.
(L) **Lunching Light**—Eat light lunches. Heavy midday meals make you sluggish during the afternoon.
(M) **Managing Calls**—Return calls just before noon or just before 5:00 p.m. each day. This may help prevent the other person from rambling.
(N) **Nagging to Motivate**—Don't be afraid to do some gentle nagging if someone else's work is delaying one of your projects. The squeaky wheel really does get the grease.
(O) **Optimizing Errands**—Link your errands. Instead of four trips a day, go out just once and stop at the dry cleaners, library, bank, and grocery store.
(P) **Planning Success**—Plan your work and work your plan.
(Q) **Quitting Meetings**—Avoid meetings whenever possible. If you must convene a meeting for some reason, prepare a specific agenda ahead of time and stick to it.
(R) **Rewarding Yourself**—Instead of punishing yourself for wasting time, give yourself rewards whenever you manage time wisely. Reinforce your successes in positive ways.
(S) **Subduing Distractions**—When you are home and need to concentrate, use ambient noise (the hum of a dehumidifier or music playing low) to subdue distracting noises.
(T) **Tasking Efficiently**—Combine tasks whenever possible. Organize your desk while talking on the phone. Shine your shoes while watching the evening news on TV.
(U) **Using Power Naps**—Keep in mind that short "power naps" provide bonus energy for the body. Lay your

head down, clear your mind of all thoughts, breathe evenly, and doze off for a few minutes. You'll awake refreshed.

(V) **Valuing Privacy**—When it comes to bookkeeping, accounting, business correspondence, or company public-relations work—all tasks that call for serious concentration—protect your privacy. Do away with the open-door policy.

(W) **Winning with Your Strengths**—Never consider defeat. Concentrate on your strengths, not weaknesses.

(X) **Examining Your Errors**—Learn from your mistakes, so you don't repeat them.

(Y) **Yielding to Change**—Anticipate change, prepare for it, and adapt quickly when it comes.

(Z) **Zapping Parkinson's Law**—Remember Parkinson's Law: "Work expands to fill the time allotted for its completion." For this reason, set challenging deadlines.

Biblical Views of Time

An old joke relates well to the misconception many people today have about time management. It seems that one day a man was driving by an apple orchard when he happened to see a farmer lifting his pigs one at a time up to the tree branches so the pigs could eat the apples. The man stopped his car, got out, and approached the farmer. "Excuse me," he said, "but isn't that an awfully time-consuming practice?"

The farmer looked at the man, shrugged, and said, "So what? What's time to a pig?"

Whereas the absurdity of the farmer's situation in this story is obvious, situations that are equally absurd, yet not nearly as obvious, exist in countless businesses, churches, and families today. It behooves the time-conscious person to examine his or her time management practices to make sure they are functional and practical. The greatest desire in the world to be a hard worker is of no value if a person's work is simply wheel-spinning rather than forward motion.

The Bible has much to say about the proper use of time. The first directive from God was to "subdue the earth." You can't do much subduing if you are not time-conscious and focused. The apostle Paul was blunt in regard to an individual's obligation to help at subduing. He wrote in 2 Thessalonians 3:10, "The one who is unwilling to work shall not eat." Fifteen centuries later Captain John Smith instituted the same rule when he and his followers set out to build a colony in Virginia. People who use their time wisely are able to reach incredible goals.

The Old Testament teaches an interesting, if subtle, lesson about time management. About one year after Moses had led the children of Israel out of Egypt and into the desert, he was instructed by God to count all the people. Surely, with worrying about hot days, cold nights, low rations, lack of water, attacks from enemies, and general organizational problems, Moses didn't need any new headaches.

Nevertheless, Numbers 1:1–2 says, "The LORD spoke to Moses . . . in the Desert of Sinai on the first day of the second month of the second year after the Israelites came out of Egypt. He said: 'Take a census of the whole Israelite community.'"

A few verses later we read this interesting passage in Numbers 1:17–19: "Moses . . . called the whole community together on the first day of the second month . . . And so he counted them in the Desert of Sinai."

Did you follow that? Moses was already greatly burdened with problems. But when given a new challenge, he began to work on it *that very day!* He didn't waste time complaining or making excuses or setting up a committee to study the available options. He got to work and completed the job. His mission was accomplished, his task completed, his goal obtained. Procrastination was not part of his makeup.

If I've learned anything from the wisdom accumulated throughout the ages, it has been that time passes quickly. King David wrote, "You have made my days a mere handbreadth; the span of my years is as nothing before you" (Psalm 39:5). In another psalm we read of our days, "They are like the new grass of the morning: In the morning it springs up new, but by evening it is dry and withered" (Psalm 90:5–6).

Perspectives on Time

Each person has his or her own way of perceiving time. A pilot was once flying near the airport in Nashville. He called the control tower and asked, "What time is it?"

A voice responded, "That depends on which airline you're with."

"What!" said the pilot. "That's ridiculous! What difference does it make which airline I'm with? I just want to know what time it is."

"Oh, it makes a lot of difference," said the voice in the tower. "You see, if you're with United Airlines, it's zero-eight-hundred hours. If you're with Delta Airlines, it's eight o'clock in the morning. But if you're with Fred's Crop Dusting Service, the big hand is on the twelve and the little hand is on the eight."

Indeed, how we look at, perceive, and value time makes all the difference in how we handle time. The main thing to remember about developing time-management skills is that you cannot begin any sooner than now. There is no profit in hiding behind clichés such as "time flies" and "there aren't enough hours in the day." Actually, there are plenty of hours in the day. I can prove it.

Let's suppose you have a secret ambition to become a gourmet cook or to write a novel or to make a hand-crafted quilt or to become a ventriloquist or to learn to speak Italian. You haven't pursued your dream because, well, there "hasn't been enough time." Still, you hope that perhaps someday . . .

Well, guess what? I now can make your dream come true in just one calendar year. That is, if you really want to devote a little time toward realizing your goal. And the best part is that you can keep your regular job, still get plenty of sleep, and not interfere with your weekends.

What you need to do is set aside two hours per day, Monday through Friday, to devote to your goal. It will probably mean doing away with coffee klatches, evening television, and some other nonessential activities you now engage in on a regular basis. But it will be worth it.

Each day has twenty-four hours. You can sleep eight hours, work at your regular job eight hours, and then use six hours for any activities you wish (eating, reading, helping your kids with their homework, exercising, shopping, mowing the lawn, cleaning the attic). But save two hours per day, Monday through Friday, for your special project. Don't be afraid to juggle your schedule to meet the challenge. Do your project from

TIME MANAGEMENT CONCEPTS SHARED BY JESUS

6:00 to 8:00 in the morning (before the family rises) or from noon until 2:00 in the afternoon while the children are down for a nap or from 9:00 to 11:00 at night when everyone else is in bed.

Here's what will happen. At the end of one week, you will have spent ten hours working on your special project (5 days x 2 hours per day). At the end of one month, you will have logged a regular forty-hour workweek on your project (4 weeks x 10 hours per week). At the end of one calendar year, you will have logged three solid months of forty-hour workweeks on your project (40 hours per month x 12 months = 480 hours = 3 months).

Let's face it. If you cannot learn to make some gourmet meals or rough out the first draft of a novel or be able to carry on a basic conversation in Italian after 480 hours of practice, you just aren't trying.

Within a mere three years of ministry, Jesus trained disciples, preached sermons, healed the sick, traveled to a number of cities, debated with religious and political leaders, blessed children, spent quality time in prayer with his heavenly Father, showed respect to his mother, evicted the moneychangers from the temple, fed the hungry, and raised the dead.

How about you? Are you using your time wisely?

Judas fought his way through the melee of flying Frisbees, clowns on stilts, ring toss games, picnic blankets, barbecue grills, and horseshoe pitchers. Finally, he made it to where Jesus was seated amidst a large group of youngsters. Jesus had a puppet on each hand.

"Oh, my son, my son, you've come home at last," Jesus said, as he moved the two puppets together in an embrace. "Hurry, servants! Get a robe for my son and new sandals and some rings for his hands."

Judas looked at his watch, wondering how long it would take for the story to end. He shifted his heavy briefcase to his left hand and pulled at his tie.

"Lemonade?"

Judas flinched. "What?" He turned abruptly.

Pete Fishers held out a glass and asked, "Care for a glass of lemonade? You gotta be hot, coming to a company picnic wearing a three-piece suit."

"I am not part of this picnic," said Judas, nevertheless accepting the proffered lemonade and taking a large swallow. He grimaced. "Ugh! Too tart!"

Pete smiled. "And here I thought you were born to drink the bitter cup. What're you doin' here, anyway?"

"I'm trying to keep us afloat. While the rest of you have been cavorting and frolicking around this park, I've been at the office trying to come up with some ideas for the new ad campaigns. If I can just get him to sign off on a few things, I can go back and get things started."

"Well, you're going to have to contend with his fan club. Listen to that applause! They love his stories."

"Time for intermission," muttered Judas. He weaved awkwardly through the maze of seated children until he reached Jesus. "Please, sir, a quick word with you before you engage in another saga."

Jesus looked happy. "Kids, say hello to Uncle Judas."

In unison the group chanted, "Hel-lo, Un-cle Ju-das."

TIME MANAGEMENT CONCEPTS SHARED BY JESUS

Not amused, Judas faced the children and said, "You need to run along now. Uncle Ju—, er, I have some important matters to discuss with Mr. Storyteller. You can come back later."

"We want another puppet show," protested a pigtailed girl to the left.

"I want another story!" demanded a chubby red-haired boy up front.

"Me, too! Me, too! Me, too!"

Jesus held the puppets out to Judas. "Here. You tell a story."

Judas narrowed his gaze. "Sorry. I don't tell stories. I count money. And we won't have any if we don't come up with ad campaigns for our new products. Can't you shoo these . . . these . . . little people away for a while?"

"Send them away? Not a chance. They might be just the help you need. Haven't you ever heard of wisdom out of the mouths of babes?"

"No, frankly, I haven't. And if you could just pul-lease give me half an hour of adult *wisdom, I could move forward on some projects."*

"How about a hot dog?" suggested Jesus.

"Thank you, no. I'm not hungry," said Judas. "Besides, I don't eat . . ."

"They're all-beef," said Jesus.

Judas pulled an ice chest up next to Jesus and sat on it. "I don't want a hot dog. I don't want any lemonade. I certainly don't want any children. I just want your feedback on my advertising initiatives for our new line of products."

Jesus signaled for a little boy and girl to come and sit on his lap. "Okay, Uncle Judas, you talk, and Ming and Klaus and I will try to help you."

Judas sighed heavily. "Can't you take this seriously?"

Jesus looked Judas straight in the face. "Trust me," he said, "whenever I have any dealings with you, I'm deadly serious." He waited a beat, then smiled and said, "So, proceed."

Frustrated, but sensing he was out of other options, Judas opened his briefcase and extracted a stack of photos showing pieces of furniture. Each photo was encased in a plastic covering.

"Until now, we've concentrated on heavy outdoor wooden products—deck chairs, work benches, picnic tables, lifeguard towers . . ."

"I know our catalog," said Jesus softly.

Judas paused. "Yes, yes, of course. Now, however, we're expanding into indoor products. You've seen these photos of the high chairs, rocking chairs, dining room tables, children's toys."

"I helped design some of those products."

"Hmmm, so you did. I've always said, you can take the carpenter out of the sawdust, but you can't take . . ."

"What is it you want?"

Judas leaned closer. "A new marketing strategy. In the past, distributors have come to our warehouses, looked at our models, and placed orders for their stores. We experimented with having a sales rep, Jon Markelson, reverse the process and actually make calls on the distributors, That proved to be so-so at first, but Jon has started to show some promise, so we may try a few other reps eventually. However, for now, we need to figure out how to get directly to the consumers themselves."

"I'm sure you have a plan."

Judas pulled a tablet from his briefcase and tapped the screen to life. "I do. Social media targeting. We'll customize ad placement on Web 2.0 platforms to create a nationwide buzz for our new furniture line."

TIME MANAGEMENT CONCEPTS SHARED BY JESUS

"Our Web site already gets thousands of visitors every month," Jesus pointed out. "From all over the world."

"That static site is so yesterday it doesn't bear discussing," said Judas with an arrogant sneer. "I'm talking about using profile data from social-networking media to deliver ads directly to individual users whom we've matched to our specific target group." He held up the screen for Jesus to see. "Here's a great example that uses an animated show-biz model."

Jesus ignored the tablet. "Ming, if you get a new toy you really like, and you want everybody to know about your toy, what do you do?"

The little black-haired girl grinned and revealed two missing front teeth. "I bring it to school for show-and-tell," she answered. "My teacher let me take my dollhouse to the front of the room and open it and take out all the people."

"Brilliant," said Jesus. "Absolutely brilliant. There you have it, Judas."

Judas sat perplexed. "There I have what?"

"Your new marketing strategy," said Jesus. "Use show-and-tell. Prepare catalogs that show the products and describe them and list their prices. Recruit a nationwide team of people to put on home-demonstration parties. For a modest wholesale cost, we can supply the samples of our toys and children's rockers and other items. They can show the products and take the orders. Once customers learn to appreciate a few of our smaller products, they'll be prone to order our larger products. Good ol' show-and-tell."

Judas sat back and mentally weighed all he'd just heard. *It's childish in its simplicity, he thought,* but if Tupperware and Shaklee and Amway and Home Interiors have succeeded at it, then why couldn't . . . ?"

"*I truly hate to admit this,*" Judas told Jesus, "*but that is a rather good idea.*" He began to type a memo to himself on his tablet.

"*Anything else?*" asked Jesus.

Judas looked up. "*Uh . . . yes . . . there is the matter of compensation for the sales force.*"

Jesus looked at Klaus. "*Do you get an allowance each week from your parents?*"

"*Yes. I get two dollars if I make my bed, clear the table each night, and help watch my baby sister.*"

"*But, what if you need more money?*" asked Jesus. "*What if you want to save up for a special toy or game?*"

"*Well . . . sometimes I can help my grandma pull weeds in her garden. And sometimes I help my grandpa wash his car.*"

Jesus nodded approval. "*Very good, Klaus.*" He looked at Judas. "*Did you get all that?*"

"*All what? Garden weeding and car washing?*"

"*You're missing the point,*" said Jesus. "*Even a child can figure it out. You provide a base payment for all the sales reps to cover their gas mileage and usual overhead. Call it their allowance. Then, when they make sales, they get commissions.*"

"*The more cars they wash and weeds they pull . . .*"

"*Exactly.*"

Judas pushed his charts and photos haphazardly back into his briefcase and stood. "*I have what I need. I'm going back to the office.*"

He turned and started walking toward the center of the festivities.

"*The office is the other way,*" called Jesus.

Without turning around, Judas said, "*I'm getting a hot dog.*"

Section 10

Jesus on Humility, Accumulation, and Independence

Man created the Tower of Babel; God created new languages. Man designed an airplane; God designed eagles, cranes, and hummingbirds. Man built the *Titanic*; God made the iceberg.

Man's greatest efforts have always been utterly puny when measured against God's wonderments. Mark Twain was correct when he noted, "Man is the only animal that blushes—or needs to." We have so much to be humble about. Even our personal righteousness is nothing more than "filthy rags" apart from the cleansing power of Christ's blood, shed on our behalf.

Ironically, it is usually people of great prestige and status who are most aware of the awesomeness of God and the minuteness of man. King David, Israel's mightiest military leader and astute statesman, saw himself as merely a speck on life's continuum. He often fell to the ground and cried aloud to God, seeking mercy and asking for wisdom. David had learned the value of a humble heart.

But what are the lessons of humility? Jesus himself bent before each of his disciples and washed their feet, then dried them with the towel hanging from his waist. Peter, in his zeal to show love for Christ, refused to let Jesus wash his feet. But Jesus insisted. There was a lesson to be learned.

It had been a requirement in the days of Aaron and his sons that when they approached the holy tabernacle of God as priests, they had to wash their hands and feet (Exodus 30:17-21). Failure to complete this symbolic cleansing resulted in death.

When Jesus came to Earth, there no longer was a need for a tabernacle. God was there, in the flesh, among men and women. The holiness of the tabernacle was embodied in the holiness of Jesus. It was still appropriate to approach this holiness in a state of cleanliness. Yet, note the difference: the Holy One was, himself, assisting the unclean worshippers in cleansing themselves.

"I have set you an example," Jesus explained, "that you should do as I have done for you" (John 13:15).

And what had he done? He had used humility rather than pride to demonstrate love and devotion to his followers. He had brought twelve people to a state of cleanliness—not just for their physical benefit but, more importantly, for their spiritual preparedness in seeking God. Jesus had shown devotion to his heavenly Father by putting himself in the role of a servant ready to do his Father's will.

If the disciples could emulate this behavior in their actions toward one another, they would always remain a team (v. 14). If they could show humility in serving others in the world, they would fulfill their commission from Christ (v. 17). If they could be so Christlike as to get strangers to accept Jesus by virtue of

JESUS ON HUMILITY, ACCUMULATION, AND INDEPENDENCE

the love they showed each other, they would bring glory to God (v. 20).

So Christ demonstrated that one of the greatest aspects of leadership was to have a willingness to be a servant. "Anyone who wants to be first," explained Jesus, "must be the very last, and the servant of all" (Mark 9:35).

Understanding the Concept

A story is told of a pompous sergeant during the Revolutionary War who ordered a lowly private to move a heavy log to help prepare the American defense line before a battle. The private pushed and tugged and struggled, but he could not carry the log by himself. After a time, a wealthy gentleman dressed in an expensive cape and new black boots rode by on a white stallion.

"Shouldn't you help this man move the log?" the gentleman asked the sergeant.

"Out of the question!" roared back the sergeant. "I'm a noncommissioned officer! I'll not dirty my hands in common work with a mere private!"

Hearing this, the gentleman dismounted his horse. He grabbed one end of the log and lifted it. The private grabbed the other end and together they carried it to the barrier.

"Thank you," said the private. "I appreciate your help. Tell me, sir, what is your name?"

The gentleman threw back his cape and revealed the uniform of a general. "Washington," he said. "George Washington." And with that, a great cheer rose from a nearby group of enlisted men.

Mother Teresa spent her adult life caring for the homeless of India. She sought no personal recognition or any special rewards. Upon receiving the Nobel Peace Prize, she used the cash to pay for more hospital supplies for the clinics she directed. Her face was on the covers of world magazines, yet she went about her days laboring as a nurse, bookkeeper, cook, waitress, janitor, and prayer partner. Her consistent dedication to caring for the poor and needy resulted in the saving of thousands of lives.

If we looked for a common denominator that linked people as diverse as a nun like Mother Teresa and a combat leader like George Washington, we would find at least one specific similarity. Both of these people were completely dedicated to a cause they deemed so noble as to merit their total commitment. No sacrifice was too great, no challenge was too difficult, no work was too demanding or demeaning. These people were so gratified to have been allowed to serve using their capabilities—and thereby fulfill their personal senses of destiny—they were willing to do anything to see the cause reach success. It was the *noble cause* in each instance that counted, not the fame of the worker.

This is exactly the sort of total dedication to "the cause of salvation" Jesus evidenced throughout his ministry. "Not my will, Father, but yours," was his humble prayer.

The Humility of Christ

In all he did, Jesus showed humility. He walked with royalty and commoners. He ate with the righteous and the unrighteous. He did not condemn the prostitute but rescued her, then absolved her, and helped her begin a new life. He welcomed the little children to come near him. He obeyed the request of his mother when the host at a wedding in Cana ran out of wine. He rejected Satan's offers of possession of earthly kingdoms.

Jesus was totally dedicated to his mission. It was the cause that mattered, not his personal glory during his brief time on Earth. One day he would sit at the right hand of the Father, but for those few years, commitment to the work at hand was all that mattered. He was willing to do anything in his power to fulfill the Old Testament prophecies and to redeem mankind.

We, too, should be willing to put aside personal vanities and, instead, emulate the Master who taught us, through his walk, to be humble.

The apostle Peter was a quick-tempered, rowdy, loud-talking man. After serving as Jesus' disciple, Peter's manner changed. He became tolerant, forgiving, and gracious. He used Christ as his example and was able to maintain this transformed life. As late as forty years after the crucifixion of Jesus, Peter was still teaching his fellow Christians, "Clothe yourselves with humility toward one another, because, 'God opposes the proud but shows favor to the humble.' Humble yourselves, therefore, under God's mighty hand, that he may lift you up in due time" (1 Peter 5:5–6).

God's hand is still mighty, and so are his deeds; and the greatest of his deeds is the creation of his plan of salvation. Knowing that it is available to us for the asking should humble us all.

We Still Can't Take It with Us

Humility is not something that comes naturally, and this is especially true in nations where free enterprise, entrepreneurship, and business acumen are lauded. Successful individuals usually discover that financial greatness can lead to a false pride. It is transparent and unrewarding in the long run. In the movie *Wall Street*, the central character, Gordon Gekko, proclaimed, "Greed is good." For a time, it seemed that this mantra was working for him, but, in time, he lost all his friends, lost all his money, and was sent to jail. In the movie's sequel, *Wall Street 2: Money Never Sleeps*, he is finally released from prison. Gekko lectures on a college campus, where students poke fun at him for his former credo, and he admits it "cost" him greatly.

The question then arises as to whether people can become very successful, yet not let greed and ambition dominate their lives. I truly think it's possible. I think this because of a role model I had in life.

My father was a self-made man. From an eighth-grade dropout, he rose to become president of three successful businesses. He believed that a bit of struggle in life wasn't so bad—it built character. And, to that end, he claimed that when he died, his last will and testament would read, "Being of sound mind, I spent every dime I had before I died."

Now, before you begin to feel sorry for me in my sad prospects of never receiving any inheritance, let me tell you that I had always hoped my father really would carry through on his plan.

My father was a good Christian man. He gave hours of his time and a great deal of his money in support of orphanages, schools, churches, and worthy civic causes. The Lord, in turn, blessed my father with financial and other rewards.

If my father, after having led a "rich" life in all aspects of the word, were to have died penniless, he would have achieved the ultimate goal of a fulfilled life. Let me explain to you why this is less paradoxical than it may seem.

More Toys

From the world's perspective, the attainment of money, land, and other tangible goods is the only way to determine whether a person has been successful in life. In fact, one famous Hollywood movie star and recording artist had a separate building next to his home that contained hundreds of toy trains, miles of railroad track, and thousands of model railroading accessories. On the door to his building was a brass plate with the engraved message, "The Guy Who Dies with the Most Toys Wins!"

From a Christian perspective, nothing could be further from the truth. Jesus taught that to spend a life hoarding material goods rather than sharing with the needy was to put one's soul in an indefensible position when brought before the judgment seat of God. Thus, the guy who dies with the most of *anything* actually *loses*.

Bigger Barns

In Luke 12:16–21 Jesus told the story of a wealthy landowner whose harvests were so bountiful, his barns couldn't contain all the crops. Instead of donating the excess food to people who were less fortunate, the man ordered his little barns torn down and larger ones built. In this way, he could store all the food for himself.

That very night the man died. His soul was called into judgment. His earthly wealth and possessions were of no value to him as he stood before God.

Unspent Millions

That parable is reminiscent of a story reported in a major metropolitan newspaper in 1937, the day after John D. Rockefeller died.

Rockefeller's chief accountant was approached by a reporter who asked, "Hey! Just how many millions did old J.D. leave behind?"

The accountant joked, but with a straight face, "All of them."

How true, how true. The oft-quoted catch phrase, "You can't take it with you," is actually biblical in nature. It was Job who said several thousand years ago, "Naked I came from my mother's womb, and naked I will depart" (Job 1:21). You would think after all these years we would have learned the truth of that lesson. But we haven't.

Dangerous Riches

The same problem was true during Christ's time on Earth. A rich young prince came to Jesus one day and asked how to obtain eternal life. Jesus told him to obey the commandments. The young man said he was already doing that.

Then Jesus added that the prince should distribute all his personal wealth to the poor. This saddened the prince, for he enjoyed hoarding riches to himself.

"Jesus looked at him and said, 'How hard it is for the rich to enter the kingdom of God!'" (Luke 18:24).

What was the lesson here? That it is sinful to be financially prosperous? No, not at all. The lesson was that there is a better definition of "rich." There is nothing wrong in being financially well-to-do, so long as it does not make you spiritually poor.

JESUS ON HUMILITY, ACCUMULATION, AND INDEPENDENCE

Jesus taught that those people who make sacrifices in order to serve God *and* serve the needy will be blessed "in this age, and in the age to come" (v. 30). In other words, we get "the best of both worlds," to put it in contemporary terms.

So it is, then, that I could rejoice with my dad when he told everyone he planned to die penniless. He knew the secret: The guy who dies with the fewest toys wins!

The God-honoring balance between remaining humble while also wanting to get all we can out of life leads us to this question: What role does money (or any kind of wealth) play in the life of a Christian? The answer is, it can play a significant role, as we shall discover.

Being Wealthy Isn't Sinful, Illegal, or Fattening

If you were reared in a conservative church atmosphere where the accumulation of wealth was silently condoned but never openly endorsed, you may still be having some difficulty believing that it is, indeed, permissible for you to strive for financial independence. If you should decide to discuss this with another Christian, you will no doubt sooner or later have someone quote to you from Luke, chapter 12.

Luke 12:16–34 has been used as a screen for people of poor monetary stewardship to hide behind for many years. Unfortunately, if these people would ever really take the time to read and study this passage of Scripture, they would realize that what Jesus was emphasizing was not the merits of poverty but, rather, the necessity of keeping things in their proper order. His message stressed the point that the salvation of our souls is more valuable than any commodity, and until that is secured, all other accumulations are meaningless.

Sometimes people get confused and reverse the priorities in their lives. I've known people who have said, "I plan to become involved in the church one of these days, but right now I'm too pressed for time. I need to go to college, land a good job, work my way up the corporate ladder, buy a big home, furnish it in luxurious style, build up a fat bank account, and then secure my retirement funds. After all that, I'll have some time to serve the Lord."

Christ called this the logic of a fool (v. 20). Men and women should become "rich toward God" (v. 21) before they go seeking other riches. In his parable of the wealthy man who worried more about how to increase his profit margin than he did about laying up treasures in heaven, Jesus pointed out what a fatal mistake that man made. He died early in his life, and his soul was brought before the judgment seat, where his money could not help him.

Christ warned, "Watch out! Be on your guard against all kinds of greed; life does not consist in an abundance of possessions" (Luke 12:15). The Bible tells us, "People are destined to die once, and after that to face judgment" (Hebrews 9:27). No amount of money or possessions can buy your way into heaven. The first step toward obtaining eternal wealth—"a treasure in heaven that will never fail, where no thief comes near and no moth destroys" (Luke 12:33)—is to accept Jesus Christ as your personal Savior and to live each day under his grace and by his teachings.

Christ had no objection to people working hard for the material things of life: clothes, food, shelter. As he explained, "Your heavenly Father knows that you need them. But seek first his kingdom and his righteousness, and all these things will be given to you as well" (Matthew 6:32–33).

JESUS ON HUMILITY, ACCUMULATION, AND INDEPENDENCE

The point is that a person can be rich in God but financially penniless; conversely, a person can be a financial billionaire but a spiritual pauper. It's all a matter of priorities: *God must come first.* After establishing that fact, the way is made clear to seek the other good things in life without losing perspective of God's plan for us.

Another Look at Luke 12

When Christ sent his disciples (not the Twelve) into distant lands to carry his message, he told them, "Do not worry about your life, what you will eat; or about your body, what you will wear" (Luke 12:22). There are people today who are convinced this verse applies to all people for all times. As such, they don't bother to hold steady jobs, adhere to a family budget, or invest their earnings. They feel that this Bible verse has promised them that God will guarantee enough food to eat and enough clothes to wear. But nothing could be further from the truth. That verse applied to those same disciples who were originally sent out. Later, in Luke 22:35-38, we see Jesus instruct these same people to supply themselves with needed provisions.

It is a bizarre twisting of logic for Christians to say on one hand that God owns the cattle on a thousand hills and that those riches are the inheritance of all believers as children of God, and then on the other hand to say that a tithe to God cannot be used in more functional ways to further the kingdom of God. We see an example of the latter when David and his hungry men ate the sacrificial bread. Jesus also demonstrated a functional approach when he said his disciples were allowed to pick some grains of wheat on the Sabbath if they were hungry. The point here is, options and opportunities are to be used for personal betterment, and traditions cannot augment or replace the actual disciplines taught in the scriptures.

Where is the balance? In Luke 12:33, when Christ told his followers to "give to the poor," he was implying that a donation to the poor was a noble way to use one's money. What would be the point, however, of giving money to the needy if such people felt it was a sin to accept it? For a fact, it is not a sin to accept a helping hand. The sin is committed only when one abuses such kindness. God provides opportunities in a variety of ways, including help from charities and friends.

A story is often told of a man who was caught in a flash flood. He climbed to the roof of his house as the water continued to rise. He prayed, "Lord, deliver me from this calamity!"

In time a crew of rescue workers arrived in a launch and threw him a rope. The man threw it back and said, "The Lord will rescue me." Five minutes later his neighbor came by in a rowboat and tossed him a rope. The man rejected it and repeated, "The Lord will deliver me." Fifteen minutes went by, and a helicopter came and dropped him a ladder. The man pushed it away and shouted, "The Lord will deliver me."

Just then the walls of the house collapsed and everything was washed away in the floodwaters. The man sank and drowned. When he arrived in heaven, he confronted Jesus. "I prayed fervently to you. Why didn't you rescue me?"

"I sent two boats and a helicopter," the Lord responded. "What more did you want?"

What more, indeed? Has it ever occurred to you that you may be playing out a version of that story right now in your own life? Only the punch line needs to be changed. When you ask the Lord why he never gave you a nice home or a new car or a vacation to Hawaii or a college education for your children, he might respond, "I gave you good health, citizenship in a free country, access to thousands of books in your local library, the freedom to worship me openly. What more did you want?" What more, indeed?

Each Christian must assume a large element of responsibility for his or her own prosperity in life. God did not say to Adam, "Stand aside while I subdue the earth for you." He directed Adam to do it on his own, under the sanctions of God. That mandate is still in effect. The greater the effort, the greater the reward. The upside potential is left to the individual.

Money Itself Isn't Evil

I smile whenever a discussion begins about the risks people run of turning evil after great wealth comes their way. My longtime friend, author Jerry B. Jenkins, a hardworking millionaire, has often said, "Money only reveals who you already were." Rich people are not out at night burglarizing people's homes trying to obtain things they don't have but desperately want. Rich people are not out robbing liquor stores or mugging elderly ladies in alleys or stealing people's Social Security checks from their mailboxes.

Does this mean being rich makes one a good person? Does it mean being poor makes someone a bad person? The answer to both questions is "no." Money does not create morals, but it does remove some of the basic temptations and fills most basic needs.

It is important to remember that the Bible states that "the love of money [not money itself] is a root of all kinds of evil (1 Timothy 6:10). The warning here is that a person who devotes his or her life to amassing money just for the sake of accumulation is wasting the precious moments of life, not to mention passing up opportunities to provide blessings to others.

Still, money in a proper balance is a reassuring element in life. Remember the advice young David Copperfield received in the popular Dickens novel: "Annual income twenty pounds, annual expenditures nineteen pounds six, result happiness. Annual income twenty pounds, annual expenditures twenty pounds ought and six, result misery."

The lesson mankind has learned over and over is that happiness cannot be purchased on credit, nor can it be bought with nonexistent money. Earning substantial funds leads to the enjoyment of substantial benefits. Good people will find good uses for their money, whatever it amounts to. Anyone who tries to argue against this fact will be hard-pressed to come up with solid evidence.

One Bible verse frequently cited is Mark 10:25: "It is easier for a camel to go through the eye of a needle than for someone who is rich to enter the kingdom of God." What this verse was referring to was a narrow city gate nicknamed "Needle's Eye" because of the difficulty of bringing donkeys and camels through it when they had large baskets tied to their sides.

A God-honoring person will be God-honoring no matter his or her station in life, whether rich or poor. Nevertheless, extremes at either end will generate greater temptations. As such, it is dangerous to become obsessed with hoarding wealth for no purpose, and it is equally dangerous to be so poverty-stricken you feel driven to cheat or steal just to survive. We need balance—a balance secured by keeping the priorities and perspectives taught by Christ.

Make no mistake about it, money is just as important to Christians as it is to anyone else. In fact, our views on stewardship, tithes, offerings, and personal accountability will shape much of our behavior and our outlook on life.

If we can learn to accept this fact, then the next move is to start right now in initiating a plan of action toward accumulating more money. If you feel hesitant about this or you don't feel the time is right for you to make your move, let me see if I can change your mind. Being a procrastinator is not in your best interest (pardon the pun) when it comes to financial accumulation.

What procrastinators don't seem to realize is that delaying action will not make a job easier to perform or cause it to go away. If anything, procrastination will increase the negative aspects of a task by adding time constraints and increasing tensions.

Pharaoh suffered through ten plagues before he finally took action to release the children of Israel. Jonah tried to delay his trip to Nineveh, and God punished him for his disobedient and cowardly ways. John Mark did not attend promptly to his duties, so Paul refused to let him travel with him anymore. The Bible has no praise for procrastinators. Instead, it warns, "One who is slack in his work is brother to one who destroys" (Proverbs 18:9).

So, when should you sit in on a money-management seminar? Now. When should you begin to read books about investments, savings, leveraging, and compound interest? Now. When should you set up a family budget, establish a viable retirement account, get a will prepared, and review your insurance needs? Now. The reason Jesus focused so much on fiscal responsibility is because it is personally important. It matters to you.

Scripture teaches that the quest for financial independence is not wrong, so long as it does not take away from one's proper focus on the true riches of life. A humble spirit provides balance and focus on righteous achievements. Jesus set the example. We can make an effort to follow it . . . humbly.

The men were tired. Beyond tired. They had been working in the boardroom running the numbers, making phone calls, and cross-referencing data for more than thirty hours. Trash cans were spilling over with takeout food containers. Tablets and smartphones were turned at odd angles around the table, and a digital projector hooked to a laptop was displaying intersecting chart lines of buy-sell agreements.

"Why us?" asked Pete Fishers to no one in particular. "What'd we ever do to deserve a crash like this?"

Matt Feingold removed his glasses, pinched the bridge of his nose, then said, "For the fiftieth time, it's not just us. The whole country is in an economic downturn. It hit fast and it hit hard. We're a privately held company, so we don't have to respond to stockholders. But we still have more than two hundred fifty employees counting on us to find a way to weather this financial storm."

Andy Fishers entered the room. "I sent everyone home. Temporary layoff. Our warehouses are full, and nobody is sending us new orders. No sense in making more stuff if we can't move what we already have on hand."

His announcement generated a uniform groan around the room, but no one criticized his decision.

"Things were going so well," mused Paul Stoner, unable to suppress a yawn. He pushed his tablet away and slouched in his chair.

JESUS ON HUMILITY, ACCUMULATION, AND INDEPENDENCE

"And they will again," said Thad O'Toole. "We just need to come up with a new sales strategy."

"Sales strategy my foot," said Phil Travers, wearily. "We've polled all our outlets both here and in Canada. No one has cash flow. We've tried to speed up our developing outlets in England, Germany, France, Italy, and Japan. Same story: 'No funds for expansion at this time.' Face it, amigos, when America tanks, it sets the whole world on its ear. I'm brain dead. I have no new suggestions."

"We have our own bills that'll soon be coming due," Judas Silva said flatly. "And we all know how he feels about the workman being worthy of his hire. What's worse, besides payroll to meet, we have the lumber suppliers to worry about."

"Can we squeeze some of our deadbeat accounts?" asked Sy Zylotski.

"Don't go there," cautioned Judas with a visible wince.

"What'd ya mean?"

Judas loosened his tie. "A few months ago I asked to take out an advance on my salary so I could get a new car. He okayed it. Well, I've fallen behind on the payments the last two months. When he heard that I was squeezing our accounts for back payments, while I, myself, wasn't current with my debts, he hit the roof. I had to endure one of those 'teachable moments' that last half an hour."

"Okay, okay, somebody's got to have some kind of idea," insisted Pete. "Most of you guys went to college. Show me it did some good. Give me something fresh, something new we can try."

"Oh, give it a rest, will ya?" said Phil. "You can't make bread out of stones."

JESUS IN THE 9 TO 5

At that moment Jesus entered the room. "Maybe you can't," he said. He picked up the remote and clicked off the projector. "All right, I need you to wake up. If we're going to save this company we need to pull together as a team. I'm counting on you. I have a new game plan, so listen up."

Though groggy, the men turned their bloodshot eyes toward their CEO. A few picked up their tablets and others took a sip or two of cold coffee.

"Until a recovery kicks into gear, the old ways aren't going to sustain us," Jesus began. "Don't misunderstand me. I'm not here to do away with the old systems. I'm just going to show you ways to make them more applicable to your work . . . and lives."

The men glanced around at each other, nodded, and waited to hear more.

Jesus continued, "Our products are good, but before people will place orders for jungle-gyms and sandboxes and picnic tables, they're going to buy food, gasoline, and clothes. So, if the customers are no longer coming to us, we're going to have to go to them." He paused for effect, then added, "Globally and directly."

He moved toward a seldom-used white board and picked up a black marker. With broad strokes he made a rough outline of the eastern hemisphere. "Here are nations that need bridges, homes, schools, office buildings. We have drafters, engineers, location managers, and skilled craftspeople working for us. We'll create fifty teams of two people and send them to these countries, seeking projects to initiate and assist with."

The men were confused, not sure what he was talking about.

"Well, uh, what if they do land a contract?" asked Andy. "We can't make a profit if we have to ship heavy wood products to India or Cambodia or Sri Lanka."

JESUS ON HUMILITY, ACCUMULATION, AND INDEPENDENCE

"You're not following me," countered Jesus. "We're not going to be shipping anything. Our two-person reps are going to sell our blueprints and our structure designs, and then they're going to stay on site as coordinators until the project is done. The materials can be obtained from local vendors. We'll generate cash flow, and the local economy will be stimulated everywhere our people go."

"How do you intend to pay for all this?" asked Judas.

"Shoestring budgets," replied Jesus. "We'll send them out with pretty much the clothes on their backs. They'll have their phones and tablets with them. That'll give them access to our online catalogs and whatever else they might need, such as price lists or schematics. We'll keep a core group of engineers based here. When one of our on-site teams requests a wooden bridge to be designed, our people will go to work on it. If someone needs a barn or cabin or barracks or cowshed—or whatever—we'll meet the specifications and provide the structural layout and design."

Pete leaned forward, narrowing his eyes. "So, if I'm hearing you right, what you're saying is, back here in the States we'll keep selling direct-delivery products once the market picks up again, just the way we've always done. But, meanwhile, we're going to be selling skills-based services, such as design work and engineering and on-site management."

"That's it. We'll be taking our services to the four corners of the globe."

"Why would our people want to leave here and go traipsing off to the hinterlands?" asked Johnny Brothers. "Most of our folks have families."

"I understand that," said Jesus. "But who doesn't dream of being part of something big, something significant? These assignments will involve travel, creative construction, making a positive impact on other lands and cultures. Besides, at most we'll be asking our employees to be gone from three months to a year. People in the military take assignments far longer than that all the time."

"But what if our people arrive someplace and they aren't welcome, despite all this help and advancement we want to provide?" asked Tom Scarsdale.

"That will happen," admitted Jesus. "But the world is a big place. Our workers will just have to shake the dust off their shoes and move on to the next town or village or city. I learned a long time ago you can show some people the truth of a matter, the way they should go, and even how to have better lives, and, still, they'll reject you."

"Kicking against the goads," muttered Paul Stoner.

"Yeah, kicking," said Barney Gardner. "How soon do you want to kick this off? Are we talking right away, first thing in the morning?"

"Now," said Jesus.

The men looked at each other as though someone had just passed a death sentence on them.

"Now, sir?" asked Tom. "As in tonight?"

"The fields are abundant," said Jesus. "It's time to harvest." He pointed. "Johnny, Pete, and Jim, I want you to go to the call center. Martha's working late tonight, and when I passed the call center a few minutes ago she was putting on a fresh pot of coffee. Have her help you download our contact lists. Start calling all our employees skilled in engineering and drafting and project management. Tell them what we have in mind, and get commitments from as many as possible for short-term trips to developing countries."

JESUS ON HUMILITY, ACCUMULATION, AND INDEPENDENCE

> "It's suppertime, sir. We just sent them home an hour or so ago," said Johnny.
>
> "You're the bearers of glad tidings, Johnny. They'll be excited to hear we've come up with a plan to save the company and preserve their jobs." He looked around the table. "Paul, Tom, and Thad, I want you to start checking on the cheapest airfares you can find to . . . well, to distant lands. The rest of you, start using the Internet and your social networks, and any other sources, to discover where we would most likely be successful at finding work for our global reps. I'll be back in an hour or two, and I'll expect something tangible from all of you."
>
> "Where will you be, Boss?" asked Sy.
>
> "I'm going to my office. I'll be putting together a flow chart that will make all this continue to work, no matter who's in charge."
>
> "But, you're in charge, Boss," said Jim.
>
> "Always good to have a contingency plan," said Jesus, patting Jim's shoulder.
>
> The teams dispersed to their assigned work areas. Barney suggested making a call for some pizzas, but no one else was hungry. For a time there was chatter in the boardroom and the sound of phone ringtones . . . but after an hour or so, a stillness settled over the room. Similarly, down the hall in the call center, voices were heard and conversations were lively for about an hour. Then, the three callers decided to pause, remove their headmikes just for a couple of minutes, maybe even grab a very brief nap. Almost instantly, they were in a dead sleep.
>
> After two hours of diligent work preparing all aspects of the flow chart, Jesus emerged from his office. He was flipping a thumb drive in his hand as he walked, eager to share the information with his team. He went first to the call center and discovered

Jim, Pete, and Johnny sprawled on couches or slumped in swivel chairs, snoring heavily. He frowned. He moved down the hall to the boardroom. Paul and Barney were nowhere to be seen, possibly having gone to work elsewhere, and the remaining members of the management team were asleep. Jesus placed the thumb drive on the table. He shook his head in disappointment and sadness, turned off the lights, and walked out.

"If I can't depend on you for an hour or two . . ."

Section 11

WHAT JESUS TAUGHT ABOUT STRESS MANAGEMENT

We are all familiar with the fact that Jesus frequently "drew apart" to spend time in solitude. He would meditate, pray, rest, and strategize. He knew there were sermons to be preached, afflicted people to be healed, miracles to be performed, and disciples to be taught. Nevertheless, he *made* time to reduce the stress and strain in his life. There is much to be learned from his practices.

The Unexpected Blessings of Exhaustion

A guest soloist at our church recently opened our evening service by singing the gospel tune "Peace in the Valley." The man's slow phrasings and bass tones seemed to match the somber mood of the lyrics as he began, "Well, I'm tired and so weary . . ."

As I looked around, I saw many an individual who seemed to be both tired and weary—some abnormally so. The vocalist's song only served to make these people slump even lower into their fatigue.

JESUS IN THE 9 TO 5

Evangelist D. L. Moody once said he was tired *in* the work of the Lord but not tired *of* the work. However, my fellow congregants that night seemed to be tired of, in, on, around, and through the work. They looked whipped.

I couldn't help wondering how people who could sing "There is joy in serving Jesus" one month could be so joyless and exhausted the next. Even more to the point, I wondered how God could allow his servants to become so listless and worn out.

Oh, I knew that doctors could site numerous reasons for fatigue—poor diet, stress, viruses, toxins, depression, sugar imbalance, lack of exercise, poor sleeping habits. But to me, these people just seemed "bone weary."

A few days later an ordinary errand became an object lesson to help me think more deeply about the matter. One morning my cell phone went dead in the middle of an important business call. That afternoon I went to an electronics store to buy a replacement battery.

"You don't need a new battery," the clerk said, after checking the one I'd brought in.

"But it's dead," I insisted.

"No, it isn't," he said. "It's only discharged of its energy. Regular alkaline batteries for flashlights will go dead, but these new electronic batteries just run down. If you drain all the power from it the way you did, you can just let it sit idle for a day or two and then recharge it. You can go through three or four cycles like that before it needs to be replaced. Newer cell phones don't need batteries at all, by the way."

I found his advice hard to believe, but I decided to try it. (If it *did* work, I'd be saving six dollars.)

Sure enough, that clerk was right. I let the battery rest for two days. I then put it back in the phone one night and set it on the charger. By morning it was working just fine. It seemed contradictory, but in order to be restored to its full level of energy, the little battery first had to be totally run down and then allowed to do nothing for a while.

As I probed my Bible, I found identical situations with God's people, and I can see at least five reasons why this was probably so.

First, God can use exhaustion and weakness to remind us that our strength must come from him and not our own resources.

The apostle Paul suffered from a physical ailment that he prayed three times for God to heal. The healing was not granted, but greater grace was given Paul to endure the problem. This left Paul still weakened by the condition and all the more dependent on God for his strength. This dependence kept Paul close to God. Thus, Paul could say without irony, "When I am weak, then I am strong" (2 Corinthians 12:10).

Second, God can use exhaustion to test and then reward our faith.

After Peter had exhausted himself fishing all night and caught nothing, Jesus asked him to launch his boat again. He told Peter to cast out his nets. Peter explained to Jesus he had already fished all night, and the fish were just not there to catch. But, in faith, Peter added, "But because you say so, I will let down the nets" (Luke 5:5). Peter cast his net. As a reward for his faithfulness, his nets contained so many fish they started to break, and the boat nearly sank. It was an amazing blessing!

Third, exhaustion can serve as a reminder we need to slow down and find some quiet time to be alone with God.

As we noted earlier, even Jesus did this. After preaching all day and feeding more than five thousand people, he sent the crowds home and told his disciples to go to the next town ahead of him. He then "went up on a mountainside by himself to pray . . . alone" (Matthew 14:23). After having exhausted himself and then taking time to recover, Jesus came back to walk on the water, calm the storm, and resume his preaching and healing. On numerous other occasions, Jesus separated himself from everyone in order to rest and pray.

Fourth, God can use exhaustion to provide us with a new perspective on life.

After Elijah had defeated the prophets of Baal and had outrun Ahab's chariot, his energy was spent. He then heard that Jezebel had ordered him to be hunted and killed. He ran out into the desert and collapsed. He begged God to let him die.

Elijah was discouraged, tired, hungry, scared, and lonely. He had never felt so drained of strength in his entire life. He longed for the ultimate rest—death!

God, however, had much more need of Elijah's services, so he showed him in three different ways that things weren't nearly as bad as Elijah felt they were. God first granted Elijah a chance to sleep. Following this, food and water were provided. These two steps—securing rest and taking nourishment—did much to revive Elijah's spirits.

The third step was the most crucial of all, however: God told Elijah he was not alone in his righteous stand. There were seven thousand other people in that region who had refused to worship Baal (1 Kings 19:18). God was going to provide one of these seven thousand people to be a friend and helper to Elijah.

Elisha became the student and companion of Elijah and "set out to follow Elijah and became his servant" (v. 21). What

Elijah had originally considered to be a crushing ordeal was really just the opening of a door to an entirely new opportunity to serve. It took sleep, food, and fellowship to help him gain this new perspective, however.

Fifth and finally, a state of exhaustion can remind us of our present and future circumstances.

In this life, we must work by the sweat of our brows. Even in Christian service "the harvest is plentiful but the workers are few" (Matthew 9:37).

In many ways, life on Earth is indeed laborious and exhausting. But it's also temporary. "For in the realm of the dead . . . there is neither working nor planning," Solomon wrote (Ecclesiastes 9:10). Similarly, Jesus warned, "Night is coming, when no one can work" (John 9:4).

In the song "Peace in the Valley," the lyrics begin with a confession of weariness and weakness. They end with an optimistic look ahead to a day when "there'll be no sadness, no sorrow, no trouble . . . [just] peace in the valley for me." Our union with Christ, whether at our death or at his second coming, will begin this time of perpetual peace. Weariness now can serve to remind us of total rest then.

So it is then that exhaustion often proves to be a prelude to blessing. It can lead us to more dependence on the strength of God. It can test and reward our faith. It can draw us closer to God through prayer and meditation. It can provide new perspectives on the value of friendships with fellow believers. And it can turn our eyes toward our coming days in glory with the Lord.

So, the next time you feel bone weary, just listen for your cell phone to ring. It'll remind you that you have a rechargeable battery, too.

One More Mile

George Meegan spent seven years walking 19,017 miles from the southernmost tip of South America to the northernmost tip of Alaska. He is listed in the *Guinness Book of World Records* for having completed, in 1977, the longest continuous walking trip. When interviewed about this achievement, Meegan said, "I never thought of it as two continents. I focused only on the mile immediately ahead of me. If I ever became discouraged, I'd remind myself that I had already walked thousands of miles, so one more mile would be easy. Finally, the walk was over."

To me, the important lesson in Meegan's story is his understanding that the key to endurance is to do what you can with what you have for just a little bit longer. People often give up too quickly when only a little more effort could have led them to victory.

Roger Maris became baseball's all-time single season homerun champion by hitting just one more home run than Babe Ruth had hit in a single season.

Roger Bannister became the first person to break the four-minute mile in running. His speed of 3 minutes, 59.4 seconds was less than a 1 percent improvement over world record holder Gunder Haegg of Sweden, whose best time had been 4 minutes, 1.4 seconds.

When A. J. Foyt won the Indianapolis 500 in 1961, he was only five seconds faster than second-place Eddie Sacks, despite the fact that the race lasted more than three-and-a-half hours.

These examples—a few of many—show that just a little extra endurance can mean the difference between success and failure.

If you look for one common factor in the lives of successful people, you will find endurance—the ability to see something through to the end no matter how overwhelming the odds may seem or how great the task may be.

Jesus preached a message of endurance for his followers. He said, "Everyone will hate you because of me, but the one who stands firm to the end will be saved" (Mark 13:13).

Jesus gave a living example of endurance. He endured the rigors of his fast in the wilderness and still resisted the temptations of Satan. He endured the scourging of the whip and the tearing of the thorns and the piercing of the nails—and still fulfilled his mission of death on the cross.

Christ knew that living the Christian life would not be easy for his converts. He warned about the difficulty by telling a story about a farmer who scattered seeds all over his property. The seed that fell by the road was quickly devoured by birds. The seed that fell on the stony ground developed no roots and, consequently, it dried up in the sun and died. The seed that fell among thorns was choked and never able to grow. But the seed that fell on rich, well-cultivated soil grew to be strong plants that yielded a tremendous harvest.

Christ explained that Christians are often like the farmer's seed. If they hear God's Word while on life's wayside, Satan immediately takes it away. Those who hear the Word of God but never take it to heart are like seed on stony ground; they wither and fall prey to Satan. Thus, a lack of endurance can lead to failure in the Christian life. Jesus said that since people who are like seed on stony ground "have no root, they last only a short time. When trouble or persecution comes because of the word, they quickly fall away" (Mark 4:17). Others who hear the Word of God but never allow it to change their lives are like seed living among thorns; in time, they are choked by sin. The people who hear the Word and live by it, no matter what sort of endurance that calls for, are like the seed that fell on good soil: they grow in spiritual grace, live by the training they are rooted in, and, in time, yield great fruits of ministry.

By these examples in word and deed, Jesus taught what real endurance is: to know your mission for God and to be so convinced of its worth that no amount of criticism or personal weakness will keep you from reaching that goal.

Executive Burnout: Symptoms and Cures

We live in a fast-paced world these days. People used to wait three days for a stagecoach. Today, they get upset if their flight is five minutes late. Speed seems to be the primary concern of everyone. Fast-food restaurants, one-hour dry cleaners, and high-speed computers are routine parts of this whirlwind we call life. Is it any wonder that from time to time we "overload" our mental and physical circuits and cause burnout?

Have you ever said, "I'm not as excited about my career as I used to be"? That's a possible indication of burnout. Have you ever asked, "Why do I feel so fatigued?" or "What! Another staff meeting?" or "Who needs that client anyway?" These, too, are possible indications of burnout.

Executive Burnout Syndrome can sometimes be so advanced that it manifests physical symptoms, such as insomnia, headaches, backaches, weight loss, nervousness, and exhaustion. It can reveal itself in behavioral patterns. For example, executives who increase their rate of absenteeism, lose concern for their clients and prospects, overreact to criticism, or make snap decisions about people may be suffering from burnout. If left unchecked, this condition can also lead to relationship problems and/or substance abuse.

WHAT JESUS TAUGHT ABOUT STRESS MANAGEMENT

To be successful in life you need to have enthusiasm, optimism, individualism, and imagination. Being only human, however, you sometimes find it difficult to maintain a good and constant grip on these four factors. Life is not always manageable. Quite often, you are forced to take the bitter with the sweet. Fortunately, if you are wise enough to recognize Executive Burnout Syndrome for what it is, you can also be wise enough to overcome it.

Ten Ways to Reverse Burnout

The first two things you need to do are to get adequate sleep and to get adequate exercise. We discussed earlier about how Jesus made rest and meditation part of his life. As a carpenter, he didn't lack for physical exertion, either. The body requires rest. Don't overtax it. Luke 5:16 tells us, "Jesus often withdrew to lonely places and prayed." Going to bed a little earlier than usual, or perhaps taking a catnap on Sunday afternoons will give new vitality to your system. Similarly, a brisk half-hour walk at lunchtime or an evening or two of bowling or racquetball will add stamina to your physical makeup. If you allow your body to deteriorate, your circuits will overload with stress much more quickly.

The next two things you need to do are to make positive uses of your past and future. You should keep a log of your greatest sales days or best sermons or major deals or most enjoyable family outings or most successful operations. Read this log frequently and draw encouragement from your past successes.

Similarly, get into the habit of always planning something to look forward to and be excited about. Call a close friend and set up a lunch date for next week. Arrange a weekend of fishing for early next month. Sign up to attend a sales seminar in Hawaii next winter. Plan so you always have a future event "carrot" dangling in front of you.

The fifth tip is to study something new. Mental stimulation is a cure-all for both depression and fatigue. For example, choose a target market in your business (farmers or physicians or college seniors) whom you have never focused upon previously. Spend a lot of time and energy learning all you can about them. Read available articles and blogs. Listen to an audio series or read books about them. Talk with other professionals who are already doing such targeting and ask for their advice. Compile files in your computer on the subject. By giving yourself a challenge and by opening a new avenue of work, you will add zest and spark (and maybe income) to your life.

The sixth suggestion is for you to learn to say "no." You simply cannot be all things to all people. If you accept more responsibilities than you have time to handle properly, you will generate incredible amounts of worry, frustration, and stress. When you are approached to handle something and you do not have the time to do it, be honest and direct enough to say "no." It may be hard at first, but if you consistently remind yourself it is for your own good, as well as the good of the project you are being drafted to help with, you will soon be able to reject requests without feeling guilty. There were times when even Jesus said "no" to meeting with his family because he had higher priorities (Mark 3:31–35).

A seventh tip is for you to travel more. Burnout can sometimes be caused by boredom that is compounded by a lack of diversity in surroundings. If you've been reporting to the same office and selling in the same city for five years, plan a change-of-place activity. Contact seven potential clients in your childhood hometown and set up appointments for next week. Get out and see new faces, eat in different restaurants, travel new roads. Keep busy with your business, but don't come home for a week. After you finally do get home, plan another out-of-town selling spree for the end of next month. Keep in mind that even in work locales, variety is the spice of life.

An eighth idea is for you to develop a hobby. John F. Kennedy used to unwind by reading mystery novels. Winston Churchill found serenity in painting landscapes. Amelia Earhart liked to get involved in long games of cards. Anyone in a challenging job needs to find an avenue of escape from the "daily grind." Choose a hobby, such as stamp or coin collecting or gardening (or, as in the case of Jesus, woodworking) that will so totally occupy your concentration, you will be able to put your career in the background for an hour or two. Just as traveling to different locations can be mentally stimulating, so, too, can working on different projects.

A ninth suggestion is for you to set realistic and flexible goals for yourself. As we discussed in Section 6, goal-setting is a great idea for anyone in business; however, if your goals are not attainable or your deadline is unreasonably demanding, you will burn yourself out trying to reach the unreachable. Be a little more compassionate with yourself. Set challenging goals, but don't try to become an RN in two years or try to own your own insurance agency after one year of insurance selling. You don't need that kind of anxiety or frustration.

The final tip is for you to set up a support group of friends and peers who can offer you advice and encouragement. Do this by inviting people with common interests and objectives to a weekly or monthly rap session. Certainly Jesus spent time teaching and training the group of twelve men who followed him. Keep the meeting's tone informal, but follow a procedure each time. One meeting can be a social hour and idea-exchange session; another meeting can feature a guest speaker who will inform the group about a topic of common interest (time management, public relations, prospecting); yet another meeting can be a "confession session" in which each person tells a personal or business problem currently facing him or her and in which resolution-input from the others in the group is offered. These support groups can give you perspective on life, answers to business problems, and opportunities to fellowship.

The key thing to remember is that everyone who works hard can be a potential victim of Executive Burnout Syndrome. By incorporating some or all of the ten tips above, you can pull yourself out of the burnout doldrums or keep yourself from ever entering a career burnout phase.

Now you need to learn how to enliven yourself through a new recognition of your potential. I call it reconceptualization.

Be Transformed with a Renewed Mind

The New Testament refers to the salvation experience as being "born again." I like that metaphor because it means we can be dead to our former selves and have a new life in Christ (2 Corinthians 5:17). I am troubled at times, however, because some Christians who say they are "born again" appear to be in "an early grave." Although they breathe, walk, eat, talk, and think, they act like they are in "spiritual neutrality"—they've lost the zest of their Christianity. These folks need a lesson in spiritual and personal reconceptualization.

WHAT JESUS TAUGHT ABOUT STRESS MANAGEMENT

If you've seemed stressed, fatigued, or sluggish lately and nonchalant about your outlook on life, you could probably benefit from a bit of reconceptualizing, too. Let me explain how it's done. Whenever a marketing consultant is brought in to build sales for a business, she first reconceptualizes the business. She doesn't set about to change the business itself, but merely the way people perceive it.

And it works!

For example, a town may have seven used-car dealers but only one "previously owned vehicles" dealer; it's the latter that will attract new customers. A city may have a dozen optical stores, but only one "eye-care boutique"; it's the latter that will get all the youth-oriented business.

Can't you do the same thing? Can't you reconceive "old age" as "vintage maturity"? . . . "past your prime" as "at the summit"? . . . "youthful inexperience" as "open-minded enthusiasm"? . . . "poorly educated" as "always learning"?

Of course!

It's all a matter of discovering your strengths and capitalizing on them, and admitting your weaknesses and overcoming them. If you don't like the image you are now projecting, you can reconceptualize yourself and project a new image.

King David wrote, "What is mankind that you are mindful of them?" (Psalm 8:4). Within the unspoken response is an assumption that people are special creations, individualized beings capable of accomplishments admirable even in the eyes of the Supreme Being.

If God has given us such talents and individualized abilities, should it not follow that we should discover them within ourselves? They can be used to reshape our image, change our thinking, and give us new clarity.

In the Chinese language the character drawing for "setback" is the same symbol as the one for "opportunity." That's often true in life, too. Is that upset applecart a mess, or did you just discover applesauce? Is that piece of singed glass a ruined window, or have you invented sunglasses? It's all in how you reconceptualize things. Pray that God will open your eyes to the innovative opportunities around you.

How are you presently conceptualizing yourself? Are you naive about what you see in the mirror when it comes to wrinkles, receding hairlines, extra weight, and general grooming? Are you visualizing "ghosts" of your former self or are you seeing the real you and then capitalizing on this present "self"?

Know Thyself

To improve your life, you need an inventory of your bad habits, health weaknesses, and undisciplined behavior patterns so you will know precisely where to improve. Ask yourself the following questions. Consider your responses carefully. Be honest and realistic.

(1) Am I healthy, energetic, and strong?
(2) Do I "think young"?
(3) Am I okay with my appearance?
(4) Am I generally content?
(5) Do I eat right, sleep enough, and exercise regularly?
(6) Do others trust me?
(7) Do I act as though I like challenges?
(8) Do I appreciate the people I live with and those I work with?

Any "no" answers show an opportunity to change things for the better. Having taken the first step toward knowing more about yourself, you will begin to feel more confident. You can capitalize on this growing confidence if you will use it to become motivated. It wasn't until Jonah was motivated that he journeyed to Nineveh to preach. Once Zacchaeus was motivated, he made amends to those he had cheated.

Motivation is part of your reconceptualization process. God wants you to work, for he is with you (Haggai 2:4). You must become motivated, of your own free choice, before you can fulfill your reconceived idea of yourself. Reconceptualization is a continuous process of becoming. Knowing this, then . . .

- become aware of your true potential.
- become determined to fulfill that potential.
- become disciplined in pursuing righteous goals.
- become opportunity-oriented in serving God.
- become enthusiastic and optimistic about your ambitions.
- become more knowledgeable in your business, calling, or ministry.

Just developing the power to motivate yourself will go a long way in reshaping your image in a positive way. You'll note the difference right away. People who used to think of you as being lazy will now admire you for your drive. Folks who never asked for your advice before will now turn to you for opinions and judgments.

As you receive such trust and positive reinforcement, you will develop more energy. You will discover that your curiosity will increase in proportion to your rising energy. You will desire to learn more about everything, and you will discover that you have energy with which to do the learning.

Be informed on issues related to politics, business, science, ethics, and the arts. Be concerned about global tensions, community affairs, and family needs. Form opinions on such matters as religious freedom, sexual harassment, racial bigotry, environmental pollution, and military preparedness. Unlike the ostrich that buries its head in the sand, you must be alert, informed, and aware of the world around you.

Straight Talk

As you increase your awareness of things, you will want to share your opinions, viewpoints, and ideas with others. Enhance this by reconceptualizing your mode of talking. Instead of having people continue to think of you as a shrill-toned, idle chatterer, reconceive that image so they now will see you as a well-informed, confident speaker with a calm but strong voice. Here are some tips on how to change your way of talking:

- Avoid slang and profanity.
- Increase your vocabulary.
- Neutralize dialects and accents.
- Develop a controlled, pleasing tonal vocal quality.
- Pronounce words clearly and correctly.
- Speak in complete sentences and at an even pace.
- Maintain eye contact with your listener.

These changes in speaking patterns will assist you in becoming a more confident and dynamic person. Use your imagination to help you see a strong personal image of yourself to go with your strong, confident voice. Never sell yourself short, and never limit your potential for strength and ability. Always strive to see new possibilities in yourself. Maintain a robust faith in your new image, goals, and progress.

Reconceptualization can become like a fountain of youth. You can use your determination and spiritual strength to revamp your life as often as necessary to keep yourself happy and productive. You may wish to evaluate your life at the end of each calendar year and then plan redirections.

The reconceptualization process is systematic and dependable. Remember the procedure we have discussed: pray to God for creative wisdom; identify what and who you currently are; decide what new image you would need to project; become self-motivated to achieve this new image; expand your knowledge and awareness of things so you capitalize on your new image; speak and act properly as part of your new image.

Ever since you were a kid, you've heard people use the cliché about getting a new lease on life. With reconceptualization, you can make that cliché a reality.

Now, one final point. To help maintain your new image, you need to reduce stress. The easiest way to do that is to avoid situations that are bound to cause stress. You can work and serve, but not in ways that lead to stress and strain.

Making Service Something Joyful

One Advent season many years ago my daughter Jeanette and I had the two lead roles in the children's Christmas pageant. I played a storekeeper, and Jeanette played a youngster who worked for me. We had the time of our lives. We practiced our lines and songs together, we helped plan the designs of our costumes, and on the night of the performance, things all went very well.

For weeks after that presentation, people kept coming up to me and saying, "It was a really delightful play. And you and your daughter seemed to be having a fantastic time performing together."

I would respond, "We were having a good time. That's the key to successful service. Volunteer to do what you enjoy most."

That's one of the philosophies I've always lived by. I have given many hours of service to my church and to my community, and they've been pleasurable experiences because I've made it a habit to do what I enjoy, and then enjoy what I do. There's very little stress in that.

During the time my son was in grades one through six, I was his youth leader at church. Five boys, including my Nathan, met with me each Wednesday night to memorize Scripture verses, work on crafts, read Bible stories, and play games. When Nathan became too old for the group, I knew it wouldn't be as much fun for me if my son wasn't involved in the group. I passed on my leadership to a younger dad whose son was just entering the program. I then took on a new job as Sunday school teacher for the class my wife and I were in each week.

Whenever I sing that familiar hymn, "There is Joy in Serving Jesus," I bellow out the words. I know that joy. I have been a deacon, a lay preacher, a teacher, a youth leader, and the chairman of the school board of a Christian elementary school. I've enjoyed all these positions of responsibility. It has never been a burden for me to serve Christ in these ways; it has been a pleasure.

Conversely, if you would ever ask me to help in the nursery or lead the choir or resurface the church parking lot or offer pre-nuptial counseling to an engaged couple, I would turn you down flat. I either have no abilities in those areas or I just don't enjoy those things.

Now, you may be thinking, *Well, what if everyone thought the way you do—nothing would get done!*

I don't believe that. I think everything would get done, and done very well. The apostle Paul wrote, "There are different kinds of gifts" (1 Corinthians 12:4). He explained that the Holy Spirit enables some to preach, some to teach, some to evangelize, some to help. The secret to enjoying your service to Christ is to recognize your gifts and then to use them to his honor.

When Jesus selected his twelve disciples, he created a cooperative team. Some were scholars who could read and write; some were financial managers; some were laborers who could sail and fish, mend nets, or make tents. Together, with each man doing what he was best at, they were able to travel and spread the gospel.

Did Jesus ever ask Matthew or Judas to gather fish? No! Did Jesus ever ask Peter to manage the group's money? No! He called them to give their natural talents to his service. Interestingly enough, as I pointed out earlier, by just being together for three years, the men did learn much from one another and were able to expand their range of talents and abilities. As their talents expanded, so did their ministries. And so did their joy.

Perhaps you have wondered from time to time why God has never called you to a great ministry for him. The answer may be that he first wants you to discover the joy of service at a beginner's level, without stress and strain in trying to do something beyond your current capabilities. He wants you to be part of the cooperative team, not the solo worker responsible for carrying the entire burden.

Discover your gift. Use it. Share it.

Then get ready. It won't be long before you'll discover you've been blessed with yet another gift. And won't that be even *more* enjoyable?!

Remember, a key to managing stress is understanding that stress is a natural part of life. Undue stress, however, is harmful to us physically and mentally and emotionally. Jesus gave us many options for dealing with this. We can insist on times of rest and seclusion. We can become more positive-minded about the things that weigh on us in life, including our opinions of ourselves. And, we can find ways to serve God and to serve others that bring joy to us rather than add to our stress quotient. It's time to lighten up.

It was the night before the grand opening of the International Convention of Drafters, Construction Workers, and Interior Decorators. Jesus, Jim, Johnny, and Pete were inside the convention center getting an advance look at the stages, booths, and display areas.

"Here's the schedule," said Jim, flipping through a folder. "Since you're the CEO of the Year, they want you to sit in the back seat of a large black Cadillac convertible and be driven around the arena three or four times. Music will be playing over the P.A. system, and balloons will be released as the car does its laps."

"Not a chance," said Jesus, scanning the aisles, signs, and banners. "If I'm going to go along with all this hoopla and fanfare, I'm going to be out where the people can talk to me. My only reason for coming here is to make myself available to people who want to learn about what our company has done to impact the global economy."

WHAT JESUS TAUGHT ABOUT STRESS MANAGEMENT

"So, no Cadillac, Boss?" asked Jim.

"Definitely not," confirmed Jesus. "Tomorrow morning, I want you to go two blocks down on Sycamore Street. You'll find a mint condition Dodge Colt in front of a condominium. It'll be unlocked. It's a collector's item, so when you get inside it, the owner is going to come rushing out to ask you what you think you're doing. He'll be a really short guy, wearing thick eyeglasses. His name is Zack. You tell him you want to borrow the car for a few hours so Jesus can use it. He'll give you the keys."

"You have some history with this guy?" asked Pete.

"You could say that," said Jesus. "I met him about six months ago. He was hanging off the side of a balcony when I came down the street. He knew I would be coming that way, so he perched up there to get a look at me. He almost fell off the ledge when I looked up and called out his name. Scared the daylights out of him."

Pete shook his head in amusement. "You get a kick out of doing stuff like that, don't you?"

"Actually, I do," admitted Jesus. "At any rate, I went up to his apartment, he ordered some delivery lunches for us, and we had a good talk. When we finished, he decided to divest himself of some of his assets . . . to reallocate them to worthy charities. We've kept in touch since then. We'll use his little Colt to do my laps around the arena tomorrow. It'll be less intimidating to the people and more akin to our low-key approach to business."

"The convention directors will want you to get out of the car and work the crowds for a while," said Johnny Brothers. "They fixed up some kind of special booth just for you, where people can come by, get photos made with you, ask questions, pick up our company catalogs. You know the drill."

Jesus squinted slightly. "Special booth? Where? I thought we'd be using our own display setup."

Jim rustled through papers in his folder. "Uh . . . aisle 6, booth 66. Says here there are tables and . . ."

Jesus was already moving toward aisle 6. The three other men hurried to catch up. As the group rounded a corner, each man stopped, frozen, stunned by what he saw.

"They've got to be kidding," said Johnny. "Who authorized this?" He pointed at the display booth that sported a large red banner with their company name and logo.

"Not me!" chorused Jim and Pete defensively.

"And certainly not me," said Jesus, through clenched teeth.

Slowly, the men approached the wide display area. Their mouths hung open as they looked at Photoshopped pictures of Jesus standing between two young women wearing scanty bikinis. A placard to one side said, "Get your photo made with Jesus: Only $20."

Stacks of the company's year-end report had been reproduced, sealed in plastic bags, and marked with price tags of $5. A continuous-loop DVD was playing scenes of Jesus at work sites around America and in foreign countries; below it was a sign reading, "See Jesus in action—building, selling, expanding—Only $29.95."

Johnny Brothers grew red in the face. He raised a fist. "Three years we've spent building a company known for integrity, quality, service, and humane projects. In one night these hucksters are trying to make a quick buck on all we've created. This isn't right. This just isn't right!"

"Look over here," said Pete, picking up a spiral-bound booklet. "They've downloaded some of our generic schematics for schools and buildings and they're planning to sell them for fifty bucks a stack. Can you believe the gall of these clowns?"

WHAT JESUS TAUGHT ABOUT STRESS MANAGEMENT

Jim checked the folder once again. "Boss, there are papers here with a lot of fine print. I thought it was just boilerplate jargon, but apparently when I booked us in here, I inadvertently agreed to let them market our products and services so long as they gave us a 15 percent commission. I've messed up. These guys are thieves, clear and simple, and we got suckered. They're taking everything we stand for and turning it into crass commercialism. I . . . I don't know what to do."

Jesus was livid. "I do!" he snapped.

With unexpected fierceness Jesus leaped forward, grabbed a life-size photo of himself, ripped it down, and tore it to shreds. He repeated the action until all the posters were demolished. Then he upended the tables. Monitors and TVs and DVD players crashed to the floor. Jesus didn't even look down as imploding screens sent glass and plastic shrapnel flying past his ankles. Leaping into the air, he grabbed the large banner, pulled it down, rolled it into a bundle, and stuffed it in a nearby trash can.

"Pete, you and the others gather up all these printed materials and tapes and DVDs," ordered Jesus. "Find a dumpster and pile all this stuff inside. After that . . ."

Suddenly, a burly security guard came around the corner. He bent low in a football lineman's stance and charged directly at Jesus. Pete whirled, stuck out his leg, and tripped the guard, causing him to belly flop face-first onto the tiled floor. Seeing an open box cutter on a nearby table, Pete grabbed it, jumped on the guard, and put the blade against the man's neck.

"Unless you want to go home with your ears in your pockets, don't make a move," ordered Pete, holding the man's hair with his left hand and keeping the box cutter blade next to the man's jugular vein with his right.

"Easy, Pete," cautioned Jesus, coming quickly to the site of the scuffle. He looked down at the man. "What's the problem?"

Gasping, the man said, "I'm security. We . . . saw you on surveillance cameras . . . breaking up the place. I was nearest."

Jesus motioned for Pete to release the man. Seconds later, two other guards arrived on the run. One had a can of mace in his hand and the other was holding a billy club.

"Don't move!" said the guard with the club. "We're taking you into custody."

"Nope," said Pete, "you ain't." He stood slowly, and nonchalantly began to clean his fingernails with the box cutter.

Jim stepped between Pete and the security guard. "Slight misunderstanding," he said with a smile. "This booth area has been leased by our company. I have the contract right here." He extended one of the pages from his folder. "Apparently, our advance team got the wrong information about what we wanted for our display tomorrow. We're . . . well, we're doing some last minute alterations."

"You're tearing the whole thing apart," said the guard still holding the mace can. "You're smashing everything to bits."

"Yes, well, so we are," agreed Jim. "But we're a bit pressed for time. You see, our boss here is the CEO of the Year, so we need everything to be perfect for his grand entrance tomorrow."

The guard who had been on the floor joined his three companions. Dusting himself off, he grabbed a worker's discarded towel and wiped his face. The three security men studied the face of Jesus. "He does look like that face on all the posters," one guard admitted. "But we heard that fellow was supposed to be really nice. This guy seems . . . you know, whacked out."

"Yeah," said Pete, still holding the open blade. "He carries the weight of the world on his shoulders. It can wear a guy down *after a while. Things are okay here, though. You boys can go back to your TV monitors. We're just gonna haul this stuff out of here and then be gone until tomorrow."*

The three guards looked at each other, not quite sure how to respond. The one put away his club, the other holstered his mace can, and the third just stood there looking baffled.

"By the way," said Johnny Brothers, "we're going to make a call to our home office and have our regular display booth brought here. It's a three-hour drive, and then they'll need setup time. We'd appreciate it if you fellows could get the doors unlocked once our team arrives. It'll be rather late."

"Well . . . yeah, sure, we can do that," one guard responded. "We're the night shift anyway." He once again surveyed the debris and chaos. "But don't you think this was a bit over the top, even if you do own all this stuff?"

Jesus, who had now had a chance to catch his breath, turned toward him and with a slight twinkle in his eye asked, "Haven't you ever heard the expression, 'If thy booth offend thee, pluck it out'?"

The guard backed up a step. "Say what?" He had no idea what was wrong with this fellow, but he decided he needed to put some distance between himself and this man. CEO of the Year or not, this guy was dangerous. "Sure, sure. Anything you say, pal." He stepped back even more. He reached over and took the towel from his companion's hands and began to wipe his hands vigorously. He looked to Pete, Jim, and Johnny, then added, "I'm done with you guys. You need anything . . . well, find it yourself. We'll just stay out of your way until your regular display arrives."

Pete watched the retreating figures of the three security guards. He smiled, then turned to Jesus. "So, tell me, Boss," he asked, "how do you *really feel* about this situation?"

Section 12

JESUS ON DISCIPLINE, APPEARANCE, AND PRAYER

There's an old saying that warns, "You can't tell a book by its cover." That's especially true in the business of publishing.

I was once the guest on a TV talk show where I had been asked to discuss my latest book. The book was not actually due to arrive in bookstores for another month, but advance publicity was already well underway.

The host had placed a copy of my book on a table between us so the viewing audience could see its cover as we talked. Suddenly, the host snatched up the book and said, "Well, instead of having you *tell* us about the book, why don't I just open it at random and read a few passages to the audience?"

To his shock (for this was a live broadcast), the host then discovered that all the pages were blank. The book was just a mock-up sent to the TV station by the publisher for publicity purposes only. The *real* book wouldn't be available until the following month.

I hastily explained things to the audience, but the talk show host was so flabbergasted he could barely finish the interview.

A few weeks later, once the real books arrived, I started to throw away the mockup, but my daughter asked if she could have it to use as a diary. She explained that if she used a book marked "Diary," someone might sneak a peek and discover her intimate secrets. However, if her visiting friends thought it was just one of Dad's books, no one would pull it off the shelf. Her privacy would be guaranteed. (Hmmmmm . . .)

The Great Cover-Up

Like books, people aren't always inwardly consistent with their outward appearance. For example, during the past three decades certain evangelists have been caught in worldly situations inconsistent with a Spirit-filled life. The media coverage of this has made it seem as though nothing like this ever happened before. For a fact, the problem has existed for ages.

Jesus was confronted by the Jewish holy men. They denounced his preaching, healing, and claim to divinity. To them, Jesus responded, "Woe to you, teachers of the law and Pharisees, you hypocrites! You are like whitewashed tombs, which look beautiful on the outside but on the inside are full of the bones of the dead and everything unclean" (Matthew 23:27).

Like the mock-up book, the Pharisees looked perfect from the outside. Their "covers" were attractive. Inside, however, they were void, characterless, dead. Jesus called them "frauds." They might have fooled other people, but not him. Jesus flipped open the pages of their lives and exposed their blank souls.

Similarly, the apostle Paul was brought in judgment before these same Pharisees as part of the Sanhedrin, the highest judicial counsel of the ancient Jewish nation. When Paul refused

JESUS ON DISCIPLINE, APPEARANCE, AND PRAYER

to recant his teachings about Christ being the true Messiah, he was hit in the face.

Paul looked at the high priest, Ananias, and called him a "whitewashed wall" (Acts 23:3). By this he meant that, just as rotted timber and crumbling mortar can seem to be in good shape if they are given a fresh coat of paint, so, too, did the Jewish priest seem righteous despite his decaying spirituality.

As Christians, I believe our effectiveness as witnesses would be much greater if we would concentrate on developing what is inside us rather than always worrying about our outward image.

When I was a teenager, I attended First Baptist Church of Bay City, Michigan. When the church building reached one hundred years old, it was decided it probably wasn't safe to use any longer. The congregation voted to knock down the building and construct a new church.

When the wrecking crews came, they swung a great iron ball time and again into the church walls and steeple, but the old church would not topple. Finally, some construction workers went up into the bell tower to investigate. They came down and announced that huge timbers, two feet thick, had been inserted between the double walls of brick and mortar to provide greater stability.

"This old church is built like a castle," announced the crew boss. "The only way to bring it down will be to dismantle it. It's so solidly fortified, it could have stood *another hundred years*. You folks really underestimated the internal stamina some of these old structures have."

I've known senior saints who are like that building. They may be upward in years and appear frail on the outside, but, in truth, they are still wearing the full armor of God. More importantly, their souls are firm in the faith and their testimonies are strong in the Spirit of the Lord.

The lesson here is that things aren't always as they appear to be. Something attractive might just be "whitewashed," while something outwardly aged might actually be inwardly youthful. To God, however, nothing is hidden. His Word "judges the thoughts and attitudes of the heart" (Hebrews 4:12). He sees things as they are. We would be wise to walk our talk, and talk our walk.

But how do we increase that internal strength? One way is by sealing our bond with God through prayer.

The Discipline of Praying

Not long ago, a man said to me, "I'd pray more if I believed it would do any good."

I responded, "You've got the cause and effect reversed. The fact is, you'd believe more if you would pray more."

Like this man, other people have come to me for counseling because they were despondent over the fact that God had not answered their prayers. As ridiculous as it may seem, after talking with them I've discovered that many of them never made their needs known to God in the first place. They assumed "there was no need to pray since God already knows our needs."

Indeed, God knows every need; but we were created for fellowship with him, and prayer is an important aspect of that fellowship. David understood this. He pledged, "To you I pray . . . evening, morning and noon I cry out in distress, and he hears my voice" (Psalm 5:2; 55:17).

The prophet Daniel prayed three times each day, even though it meant risking his life to do so. Solomon dropped to

JESUS ON DISCIPLINE, APPEARANCE, AND PRAYER

his knees in submission and prayed a dedication prayer after the building of the temple. John the Baptist spent a lifetime of fasting, praying, and preaching in the wilderness.

No one would deny that these men were close to God. Nevertheless, they were unassuming and humble. They poured out their feelings and thoughts to God through prayer and earnestly sought his guidance in all matters. Their conviction that their God was a caring, listening God prompted them to turn to him with an intensity of prayer. They prayed believing that God would respond.

I heard a preacher once explain the basis of prayer power. He said, "It's not the length of your prayers—how long they are. It's not the arithmetic of your prayers—how many there are. It's not the poetry of your prayers—how beautiful they are. It's not the volume of your prayers—how loud they are. It's the intensity. That's all that counts."

If we look for the ultimate example of prayer intensity, we will find it in the prayers of Jesus. He preceded all his miracles—from the feeding of the five thousand to the raising of Lazarus from the dead—with intense prayer. Nowhere is this better depicted than in Luke 22:41, 44, where Jesus prayed that his human flesh would be strong enough to face and endure the crucifixion before him: "He withdrew about a stone's throw beyond them, knelt down and prayed . . . And being in anguish, he prayed more earnestly, and his sweat was like drops of blood falling to the ground."

Such earnest prayers cannot go unanswered by a loving God. In that instance, Jesus was given the strength he requested: "An angel from heaven appeared to him and strengthened him" (Luke 22:43).

It is crucial to note two things about the example of prayer Jesus set for us in the garden. First, there is the fact that he made a personal request. He asked to be spared the pending death on the cross. In asking this, however, he qualified his request by saying that it should be denied if it was not in line with the will of God his Father. He yielded his will to the Father's.

When it was apparent the request to avoid the cross could not be granted, the second thing Jesus prayed for was the strength *to do* the Father's will. This request was granted. God has a plan for our lives that we are free to reject or submit to. Following God's leading brings us to our greatest fulfillment, although yielding is seldom easy.

The power of prayer is God empowering us to do what is right in his eyes. Thus, we must emulate Jesus in this way: by making our needs and desires known to God, but to ask that they be granted only if they are pleasing to him, a part of the calling he has for us.

I can personally vouch for the fact that yielding to God is difficult if it means accepting something other than what you have been praying for. In 1974 I suffered damage to the nerves near my left temple. My doctors felt it was probably the result of some form of post-traumatic stress syndrome related to the year I spent in Vietnam as a sergeant in the Army. The result was gross disfigurement of the entire left side of my face. My cheek sagged, my left eyelid would not blink, my lips were twisted, half my tongue was numb, and my forehead would not wrinkle on the left side. It was terrifying.

Instinctively, my prayers were for a miraculous total recovery. I prayed fervently, but no healing came. After ten days in our city hospital, I was transferred to a large university research hospital. While there, a young hospital chaplain stopped by for a visit. I told him I had prayed for my face to be healed, but there had been no improvement.

JESUS ON DISCIPLINE, APPEARANCE, AND PRAYER

The chaplain opened his Bible and spent time reading me the Old Testament story of how Joseph was sold into slavery by his jealous brothers. By the story's end, Joseph had become the second most powerful man in Egypt. When he revealed his identity to his brothers, they were sure he would seek revenge. Instead, he forgave them. When they asked how he could be so magnanimous, he explained that God had used their evil to bring about good.

"Now, you have a similar opportunity," the chaplain told me. "Life has dealt you a hard blow. Is your faith strong enough to stop praying for what *you* want and, instead, discover what good God can bring out of this?"

"But I'm paralyzed," I mumbled through twisted and numb lips.

"Just one side of your face is," the chaplain countered. "Your legs, feet, hands, arms, and back work fine, as do your hearing, thinking, seeing, and senses of smell, taste, and touch. Find out what God has in store for you. Yield to him."

From then on I changed my prayer. I continued to ask for my face to be healed, but I also prayed that if that was not part of God's will for me, then I wished for the grace to accept my situation and to serve where he could use me.

To my total amazement, the paralysis turned out to be a life-altering blessing from God. I had to attend speech therapy class in order to learn how to speak clearly again. I was given tips on vocal projection, enunciation, delivery, and body language. Soon, I not only learned how to speak again, but I also developed into a public speaker. Thanks to that training years ago, I now deliver more than fifty major speeches each year at colleges, universities, conventions, and corporations. I also teach a Sunday school class each week and make numerous guest appearances on radio and television programs. Had it not been for the paralysis, this phase of my career might never have opened itself to me.

In the years since 1974, I have regained the feeling and much of the motor movement of my forehead, nose, lips, and tongue. My eyelids and left cheek still show evidences of the original nerve damage, however. But I never think about it. If people ever ask me about it, I tell them, "It was something that seemed to start out bad, but through the power of prayer it wound up working to my good."

So, if you ever catch yourself saying, "I'd pray more if I thought it would do me any good," just change that to, "I'm praying *now*, Lord, so I can discover what *is* good for my life!"

Jesus touched the intercom button. "Yes?"

"Ah-h-h-h . . . two men are here without appointments, sir," came the secretary's voice, somewhat hesitantly. "They say they need to see you right away."

Jesus smiled. "Would that be Matt Feingold from Accounting and Pete Fishers from the warehouse?"

"Well . . . yes, sir . . . but . . ."

"You can show them right in, Martha. Thank you."

The office door flew open without any assistance from the secretary. Two men strode rapidly in, closing the door behind them. One was dressed in a white shirt with narrow blue stripes, a navy tie, dress slacks and polished black leather loafers. His hair was neatly trimmed. He was closely shaven, and he wore

JESUS ON DISCIPLINE, APPEARANCE, AND PRAYER

a pair of gold wire-rim glasses. In his hand he carried a tablet computer atop a manila folder.

The second man wore a red-checkered flannel shirt, open at the neck revealing a sweat-stained T-shirt. His faded blue jeans were cinched by a hand-tooled leather cowboy belt with a silver buckle and turquoise insets. His work boots were dirty, and the steel toe protectors were dented in several spots. He wore his hair over the collar, and his cheeks and chin carried a five o'clock shadow, even though it was only 10:15 in the morning. In his hand he carried a crumpled business letter.

"Good morning, gentlemen," said Jesus. "Have a seat."

Neither man sat.

"Boss, we need to talk about this letter," insisted Pete, shaking the crumpled piece of paper. "I mean, this don't make no sense."

"Any sense," Jesus corrected him.

"He's right," agreed Matt. "At least about this letter. You . . . you really can't mean this, sir."

"I never lie," said Jesus. "You know my policy about that."

"Well . . . yes, sir," stammered Matt. "But what I mean is, this just doesn't seem . . . well . . . productive. I'm an accountant. Why are you ordering me to spend two weeks working in the warehouse? I don't know anything about crating products and loading trucks."

"He's got that right," interjected Pete. "He'd only get in our way. He's got no experience, and he ain't got the strength it takes."

At this, Matt stared contemptuously at Pete. "I'm stronger than you think, I'll have you know. I play racquetball four times a week."

Pete smirked.

"You wouldn't last half a day on the loadin' docks, college boy. Look at your hands—no calluses. And those spindly arms of yours . . . You'd call it quits even if we let you use a hand truck for your loading."

"You're wrong," Matt shot back defiantly. "But I'm not going to argue with you about it." Turning to Jesus, he said, "I see no point in having me work two weeks in the warehouse, sir. But at least the concept of that is feasible. However, it is totally unfeasible that Fishers here could work two weeks for me in the accounting department. He doesn't know a balance sheet from a check stub."

Now it was Pete's turn to look offended. "Hey, college boy, we got a personal computer at home, and it might surprise you to know how much I know about keeping a budget."

Matt rolled his eyes. "Oh, please," he said, "spare me. Typing in a couple of numbers for your grocery money or your car payment isn't the same as preparing payroll for 218 people or filling out quarterly 941s for the IRS or . . ."

"Enough!" interrupted Jesus, raising one hand. "I'll say it again—take a seat. Both of you."

The two men looked as though they were going to try to interject one more quick comment, but the look on the boss's face made them think better of it. They both reluctantly settled into chairs in front of the desk.

"Why did you come to work for this company, Matt?" asked Jesus.

"I like it here, sir," answered Matt. "It's a good company."

"Why did you come to work for this company, Matt?" asked Jesus again, immediately.

JESUS ON DISCIPLINE, APPEARANCE, AND PRAYER

Matt looked at Jesus questioningly. Jesus only stared back as though he was expecting a better, more honest answer. Matt was unnerved by this. It always shook him, the way his boss could seem to see right through him.

Matt cleared his throat. "Well, I was, you know, very glad to get a chance to put my accounting skills to use in a growing company," he said slowly, "and the pay was very fair, and . . ."

"Why did you come to work for this company, Matt?" Jesus asked pointedly, his voice growing even stronger.

Matt swallowed hard. He glanced down at his shoes. His fingers gripped the tablet tightly. "I . . . I needed a chance to find myself," said Matt haltingly. "When I worked for the IRS, I never felt I was contributing to anything positive, anything worthwhile. No matter what I did or how well I performed, I never had a sense of pride about what I did. I had skills and experience, but I wasn't being called on to produce anything uplifting and significant."

"And what did I tell you when you came here?" asked Jesus.

"You said if I worked hard and proved to be an asset to the company, you'd give me every chance for leadership."

"And have I?"

Matt lifted his eyes. "Oh, yes, sir. I came in as head of finance three years ago, and you let me develop the whole accounting department. I've had four pay raises. You've been completely fair, sir. I didn't mean to imply . . ."

"How long did you spend creating our company's total financial system?" asked Jesus.

Matt contemplated a moment, then said, "It took three months to get the computer system online and programmed, a year to build our client database, another year to build and expand our workforce, and then eight months to develop our online catalog business."

"Do you see a problem in that?"

"A problem, sir?" Matt responded, his eyes narrowing in thought. "Why, no, sir. I've met all our goals thus far. I get along well with everyone in the department. There's no problem, sir."

"Oh, yes, there is," Jesus corrected him. "You've lost sight of why you came to this company. Your original goal was to prove how capable you were at management . . . at leadership . . . at continually doing positive work. After you completed your last project, you became complacent about advancing yourself."

Matt looked genuinely confused.

"But I'm already the supervisor," he said. "There's nothing above that."

"In finance and marketing there isn't," agreed Jesus, "but there are all kinds of higher positions in management. I need vice presidents, board members, and human resources managers. You've been locked into one responsibility so long, you've lost sight of what the rest of this company is all about. But you're going to learn. And Pete, here, is going to be one of your first teachers."

"Me?" yelped Pete, suddenly sitting upright. "Why *me*, Boss?"

"Because Matt Feingold has some things you desperately need, Pete. And you have knowledge you can share with him. You can help each other."

Pete shot a sideways glance at Matt and almost snickered.

"What's he got that I'd need?" Pete demanded.

"Several things, actually," said Jesus, slowly. "Matt has good grammar. He is very knowledgeable in regard to the company's money matters. He's a master at computers. And he's sophisticated. You don't have much in the way of any of those skills, Pete. But you will have . . . now that Matt's going to teach you."

JESUS ON DISCIPLINE, APPEARANCE, AND PRAYER

"*Teach* him?" said Matt. "What is this, sir, a masculine version of My Fair Lady? I can't reshape him. He's too far gone. Besides, why should I go to all the trouble?"

Jesus eased back into his chair. He looked at one man, then the other.

"Because," he said, "I've decided the two of you are going to be equal managing partners of this company after I leave."

About the Author

Dennis E. Hensley holds four university degrees in communications, including a PhD in literature and linguistics from Ball State University. Dr. Hensley is the author of more than fifty books and more than three thousand newspaper and magazine articles, as well as stage plays, film scripts, and songs. He is a professor at Taylor University, where he serves as director of the professional writing major. He and his wife Rose have two grown, married children and four grandchildren.

Dr. Hensley has received numerous honors including the Award for Teaching Excellence by Indiana University, the Elizabeth Sherrill Lifetime Achievement Award by the East Metro Atlanta Christian Writers, the Dorothy Hamilton Memorial Writing Award by the Midwest Writers Workshop, and the City of Fort Wayne Bicentennial Gold Medallion. In 2001–02 he was Distinguished Visiting Professor of English and Journalism at the Graduate School of Communication Arts at Regent University. In 2006 he was Distinguished Visiting Lecturer at Oxford University. In 2007 he was Distinguished Visiting Literary Scholar at Moody Bible Institute. He also has received Distinguished Alumnus Awards from T. L. Handy High School, Delta College, and Saginaw Valley State University. From 1970–71 Dr.

Hensley served as a sergeant in the United States Army and was awarded six medals for service in Vietnam.

Research by Dr. Hensley, an academic scholar, has been published in the *Pacific Historian*, the *Ball State University Forum*, *Echoes*, and the *Jack London Newsletter*. His 600-page opus, *The Annotated Edition of Jack London's **Martin Eden***, was hailed as "a masterpiece of literary analysis" by *American Literature Quarterly*. He has written six novels, including *The Gift* (Harvest House); a book on futurism, *Millennium Approaches* (Avon); several motivational books, such as *The Power of Positive Productivity* (Possibility Press); and other books on business, finance, communications, public relations, and theology.

When you buy a book from **AMG Publishers**, **Living Ink Books**, or **God and Country Press**, you are helping to make disciples of Jesus Christ around the world.

How? AMG Publishers and its imprints are ministries of **AMG (*Advancing the Ministries of the Gospel*) International**, a non-denominational evangelical Christian mission organization ministering in over 30 countries around the world. Profits from the sale of AMG Publishers books are poured into the outreaches of AMG International.

AMG International Mission Statement

AMG exists to advance with compassion the command of Christ to evangelize and make disciples around the world through national workers and in partnership with like-minded Christians.

AMG International Vision Statement

We envision a day when everyone on earth will have at least one opportunity to hear and respond to a clear presentation of the Gospel of Jesus Christ and have the opportunity to grow as a disciple of Christ.

To learn more about AMG International and how you can pray for or financially support this ministry, please visit **www.amginternational.org**.